Ethereum

The Complete Insider Guide to
Comprehensive Universe of Ethereum
that from Programming, Mining to
Smart Contracts, Investing, Trading
and Blockchain Technology

The purpose of this book is entertainment and the views and ideas in the book only belong to the author. These ideas should not be taken as expert advice and commands. The readers are only responsible for their actions for doing anything wrong after reading this book.

Only purchaser and reader are responsible to adhere to the application of laws and regulations in their state for advertising, professional licensing and business practices.

Neither author nor the publisher will assume responsibility or liability for actions of purchaser or reader. Any signal about a company, firm or individual will be purely unintentional.

Book Description

Ethereum is a new type of cryptocurrency designed to overcome the limitations of Bitcoin. It can help the developer in the easy development of new applications. The price of this currency depends on supply and demand, difficulty level, media, and price of bitcoin, scams, investors, innovation, market dilution, governmental issues and other factors.

This book is designed to explain Ethereum and its uses. You can understand the aspects of this currency along with its potential. This book is designed for informational purpose so that you can understand the role of this currency in the world of cryptocurrency. This book offers:

- Benefits of Ethereum and Blockchain
- Mining of Ethereum
- Effective Strategies to trade in Ethereum
- Different from Ethereum and Bitcoin

- Address Security Issues
- Learn to write a script for Ethereum, etc.

Read this book and understand the role and function of Ethereum in digital currency and financial world.

Table of Content

Introduction

Ethereum is a blockchain-based, public, open-source distributed computing platform featuring scripting (smart contract) functionality. In simple words, it is a rising star in the world of cryptocurrency. It becomes the second largest currency in the digital world in more than two years and spurring the rise and booming in the value of hundreds of new competitors to bitcoin. Ethereum was launched on 30th July 2015 and its value has been amplified up to 6,800% since the beginning of 2017. The current value of an ether is £358 ($480).

This open software platform is based on blockchain technology that allows the developer to design and deploy regionalized applications. After bitcoin, Ethereum is the 3rd most valuable form of digital currency after bitcoin with highest market value. Just like bitcoin, Ethereum is a public blockchain network. There are some technical differences between both currencies, such as Ethereum as well as Bitcoin differ considerably in capability and purpose. Bitcoin offers a particular role of blockchain technology and a peer to peer electronic cash system for online bitcoin payment.

Bitcoin is employed to track the proprietorship of digital currencies, and the Ethereum technology blockchain proves helpful to run the encoding for the decentralized application. In the Ethereum technology blockchain, the professional miners try to get Ether, rather than mining for bitcoin. Ether is a crypto token to fuel the network. Other than a tradeable cryptocurrency, crypto token "Ether" is used by application developers to pay for services and transaction fees on the network of Ethereum.

Chapter 1 – What is Ethereum and Blockchain Technology? Potential Benefits of Ethereum

Ethereum is a blockchain-based, public, open-source distributed computing platform featuring scripting (smart contract) functionality. In simple words, it is a rising star in the world of cryptocurrency. It becomes the second largest currency in the digital world in more than two years and spurring the rise and booming in the value of hundreds of new competitors to bitcoin. Ethereum was launched on 30th July 2015 and its value has been amplified up to 6,800% since the beginning of 2017. The current value of an ether is £358 ($480).

This open software platform is based on blockchain technology that allows the developer to design and deploy regionalized applications. After bitcoin, ethereum is the 3rd most valuable form of digital currency after bitcoin with highest market value. Just like bitcoin, Ethereum is a public blockchain network. There are some technical differences between both currencies, such as Ethereum and Bitcoin differ considerably in capability and purpose. Bitcoin offers a particular role of blockchain technology and a peer to peer electronic cash system for online bitcoin payment.

Bitcoin is employed to track the ownership of digital currencies, and the Ethereum blockchain proves helpful to run the programming code for the decentralized application. In the Ethereum blockchain, miners work to get Ether, rather than mining for bitcoin. Ether is a crypto token to fuel the network. Other than a tradeable cryptocurrency, crypto token "Ether" is used by application developers to pay for services and transaction fees on the network of Ethereum.

More Than Money

Ethereum is not only a digital currency, but it is more than just money. It is a platform based on blockchain with numerous aspects. It features EVM (Ethereum Virtual Machine), the smart contracts and utilizes its currency known as ether for peer-to-peer contracts.

Ethereum's smart contracts use applications stored in blockchain for contract facilitation and negotiation. As the benefits of these contracts, the blockchain proposes a decentralized method to enforce and verify them. Different decentralized phases make it incredibly complicated for censorship and fraud. Smart contract of Ethereum aims to offer maximum security as compared to old-style contracts and bring down related costs.

Ether powers all smart contract applications. Blackchain of Ethereum is based on crypto-currency and ether is a crypto-asset in the Ethereum wallet. It lets you use and create smart contracts. This system can be described as a solo shared computer run by the network of users and resources are paid for and parceled out by ether.

Implementation of Smart Contracts with Cryptocurrency

Ethereum enables you to produce digital tokens. These tokes are used for the representation of shares, virtual assets, proof (evidence) of membership and much more. Basically, small contracts can be attuned to wallets and particular exchanges that employ API (a typical coin). It is possible to copy a code from the website of Ethereum and use tokens for numerous purposes, such as the representation of shares, voting forms and fundraising. You may possess a particular quantity of tokens in the rotation or an inconsistent amount on the basis of predetermined rules.

Kickstarter is not Required with Ethereum

Ethereum allows developers to increase funds for numerous applications. For a new project, you will get a chance to seek inductees from the municipal and set up a contract. A fundraising will be continued until the goals are reached or a particular date. The funds are released again to the contributors if the particular goal is not fulfilled, or go on the project if it is prosperous. Kicking out Kickstarter means a 3rd party is booked along with its rules and they also charge a particular fee. It may include processing charges, Kickstarter may take almost 10% of the budget of a project.

Free from Conventional Organization Structure with Independent Democratic Organizations

Ethereum proves good to source funding and offers a legislative edifice to get an exceptional idea. You can get proposals from other people who supported your project and hold votes on the possible procedures. It allows you to skip the expenditure of a conventional structure, such as completing paperwork and hiring managers. Ethereum protects a project from external influences, while it's decentralized network make sure to avoid any downtime.

There are numerous small aspects that make both blockchain-based projects different. Average block time of bitcoin is almost 10 minutes, but the Ethereum aims for 12 seconds. This instant time is enabled by the GHOST protocol of Ethereum. A quick block time indicates that confirmations are quick. There can be more orphaned blocks. Another difference is the monetary supply of both cryptocurrencies. More than 2/3rd of bitcoins are already mined with the majority going to initial miners. Ethereum elevated its promotion capital with a presale and almost ½ of its coins. These will be minced by its 5th year of existence.

The incentive for mining Bitcoin splits almost every 4 years and it is presently valued at 12.5 bitcoins. On the other hand, the rewards of Ethereum miners are based on the proof of its algorithm known as Ethash, with five ether provided for every block. Ethash is a tough algorithm that inspires decentralized mining by folks instead of using more centralized ASICs similar to Bitcoin.

Ethereum and Bitcoin cost their transactions differently. It is known as Gas in Ethereum and the cost of transactions depends on the storage needs, bandwidth usage and complexity. In Bitcoin, the block size is important to determine the limit of transactions and they equally compete with each other.

Ethereum has its own Turing complete interior code that shows that anything may be calculated with sufficient time and computing power. Bitcoin misses this capability, but there are particular advantages to Turing-complete. Its complications may bring security complexity that contributed to DAO outbreak in June.

Bitcoin and Ethereum are two different beasts and have their own aspects. In reality, both have particular differences and intentions. Bitcoin emerges as a steady digital currency, and the Ethereum aims to incorporate more, with ether is just a component of smart contract applications.

Understand Blockchain Technology

Blockchain technology has the capability to optimize the universal infrastructure to deal with universal issues in a particular space. Nowadays, everyone is talking about blockchain because this concept has keyed up a commotion in the financial industry.

The blockchain is considered as a public ledger of all bitcoin transactions that have ever been performed. One block is an important part of blockchain to record some or all current transactions and after completion, these all go into the blockchain as a permanent database. Bitcoin is a ground-breaking payment network and a unique kind of money. It uses peer-to-peer technology that works without financial authorities and central banks to manage transactions and bitcoins are issued collectively by a network. This currency is an open source and it is available to the public. Blockchains technologies are used to control and record the transaction of bitcoin and Ethereum.

Once an existing block completes, a new block will be generated. These blocks are closely linked to each other similar to a chain in a proper linear and chronological order. Each new block contains a dash of the previous block. In order to use traditional banking as an analogy, the blockchain has a history of previous banking transactions. You can find bitcoin transactions in a chronological order, similar to bank transactions. Blocks can be taken as individual financial statements. Blockchain has a complete record of every transaction of bitcoin. It provides insight, facts, the value of patents and other essential points.

Some developers believe in starting looking at the creation of various blockchains because they don't want to depend on a solitary blockchain. Sidechains and parallel blockchains will be helpful for tradeoffs and enhance the scalability with the use of independent and alternative blockchains. It will increase the chances of innovation.

Example of Blockchain

To understand the blockchain concept, there is an example of a product known as Gyft. It is an online platform to sell gift cards where the customers can redeem, buy and sell gift cards. This business is a partnership between a 44-year old merchant or FinTechn organization First Data and the infrastructure of blockchain provides Chain to provide gift cards of SMBs with the help of blockchains. This product will be rolled out and become a solid example of blockchain-based modernism that has no connection with bitcoin. It is considered as a part of blockchain because a majority of SMBs doesn't have any gift card program and POS that are installed at SMBs may not accept them.

It is really expensive to offer a program for the gift card and hard to notice the immediate benefits. It can postpone fulfillment for a retailer, but large retailers can understand it in a better way or accept gift cards. Blockchain enables Gyft to offer a gift card solution for the customers of SMB.

Non-reputable pseudonymous transaction requests

It is difficult to testify the authentication of a party demanding claim on the digital currency bitcoin. There should be a system to know the actual status of the transfer. The bitcoin blockchain is answering all these questions. Bitcoin blockchain promotes the use of arithmetical signature algorithms to solve some important issues regarding identity, authenticity, and ownership. This information is required to transfer bitcoins. In the absence of DSA, you are in need of a chief authority to manage credentials of every party and authenticate each transaction on the behalf of parties and recipients have to trust the 3rd party about the validation of transaction.

While using "DSA/cryptography" the details should be verified, such as for define hash of payload that needs to be signed, which includes having a well-defined serialization schema for its messages. As well as well-defined representations for signed messages. The information can be accessed in the blockchain block.

A domain model that fits the problem need

If one ledge contains events for state transitions in the domain model, in this case, the bitcoin needs a particular state transition. It is an ability to move a bitcoin from one place to another.

An algorithm to generate and distribute the supply of Bitcoins – eminently attained by gratifying miners who participate in the P2P network by evidence of the work, angling it towards key adopters to bootstrap the network.

You can get the advantage of future proofing to some extent by implanting the deduced scripting linguistic in the business scheme to design the most complex transfer contract.

There are a few things we can observe from these innovations. Firstly, each of these 3 problems that were solved could have been solved independently.

Bitcoin is not the only system that has Byzantine fault tolerance and these systems may not use cutting-edge cryptography or work with cryptocurrency. Many high availability systems use similar consensus algorithms such as PAXOS to achieve a consensus in a distributed ledger.

Careful use of digital signing can be used in isolation, as it does, for example, in the signing of digital software by publishers to achieve the non-repudiation of the software it publishes (i.e. Microsoft really was responsible for that update) and for clients to know it can be accepted (so auto-update can safely run on your PC). A ledger is not required for any domain logic. It's just saying the software you have really is from whom it came from.

As for the domain model, the government can replicate the capability of bitcoin by just keeping all protocols and transfer rules same, but run it on its own private servers. You authenticate through their servers to check balances and make transfers. It is basically Paypal or you may prefer Bitcoin for everything including crypto and Byzantine error tolerance, but change the rules for the distribution of coin, such as give it to yourself to start a ripple.

One final note on the scripting. The effort most famously taking this to the next level is Ethereum where smart contracts are being built on their blockchain. But hopefully, the Ethereum realizes that they are increasing the capability of bitcoin to distribute it via a P2P network, they could equally be running it as a private service to sell to clients.

The point with all this is that there is a choice in all these innovations. The blockchain is not the only solution to solve numerous problems. You need to pick and choose the pieces as you require them for your problem.

And the best example of that is Bitcoin. Bitcoin is clear on its goals to create a decentralized cryptocurrency and the blockchain technology behind it has been fitted closely to fit that goal.

Chapter 2 – The Financial History of Ethereum and Ether

At an initial level, Ethereum was described by Vitalik Buterin in a white paper. Vitalik Buterin was a programmer working on Bitcoin Magazine in 2013 and he was working on a goal to build decentralized applications. Buterin suggested that scripting linguistic is necessary for Bitcoin application development. He failed to get agreement and decided to develop a new platform with a general scripting language.

 In January 2014, the main team of Ethereum was Charles Hoskinson, Anthony Di Iorio, Mihai Alisie, and Vitalik Buterin. Formal development of this project started in 2014 through a Swiss organization called EthSuisse (Ethereum Switzerland GmbH). Afterward, a non-profit Swiss foundation (Stiftung Ethereum) Ethereum

Foundation was developed. An online crowdsale had funded this development between July and August 2014. The buyers of Ethereum got ether token with bitcoin.

Architecture of Ethereum
Presale of Ether

It is a value token of the blockchain Ethereum and listed under ETH code. It is traded on the exchanges of cryptocurrency. It is utilized to pay for computational services and transaction fees on the network of Ethereum. Tokens may be volatile as per circumstances, such as plunge of ether from $21.50 - $8 on 17th June 2016, when DAO was hacked. The value of ether had increased to more than $400 in June 2017. This rise was equal to 5,000% since the commencement of the year.

The volatility of price on a single exchange may exceed the volatility on the prices of Ether token. A "flash crash" is triggered by the large selling order on an exchange dropped the cost on that exchange to $0.10 as each offer to buy was engrossed, after which the rate quickly recovered to $300 and more.

Ethereum Virtual Machine

The EVM (Ethereum Virtual Machine) is a suitable runtime atmosphere for smart contracts in Ethereum. Buterin initiated his work with Dr. Gavin Wood to discover Ethereum. Dr. Wood released Yellow Paper Ethereum to explain the specifications of EVM. As per his papers, EVM is sandboxed and completely sequestered from filesystem, network and other procedures of the host computer. Each Ethereum in its network runs a particular EVM implementation and implements the similar instructions. EVMs have been implemented in Web Assembly (under development), Rust, Ruby, Python, JavaScript, Java, Haskell, Go and C++.

Development of Ethereum

After presale of Ether, the development of Ethereum was officially announced as a non-profit organization ETH DEV. This organization managed the development of Ethereum with Vitalik Buterin and team. The whole team of three directors delivered PoC (Proof-of-Concept) released for the growing community of Ethereum. On August 2014, the Ethereum's sale reaches to more than $14 million. In September 2014, the pre-sale investors obtained 60m Ether and 12m Ether were provided to the Ethereum's development team. The left behind ether was provided to the non-profit organization. After all this, it was October 2014, when Ethereum protocol approved five ETH cream. Rising network of miners for Ethereum and increasing traffic on the forum of Ethereum clearly defined that the network is rapidly enticing developer community.

Frontier Launch

The initial version of Ethereum was launched as Frontier on 30th July 2015. Moreover, minors were really interested and they frequently join this network to secure Ethereum blockchain and earn Ether. In fact, Frontier was the initial milestone in cryptocurrency Ethereum and intended as the beta version by developers. The release of Frontier became capable and reliable solutions and resulted in the enhanced ecosystem of Ethereum. A prearranged protocol "Homestead" was added to the network of Ethereum on 14th March 2016. In the month of May 2016, DAO set a special $150 million record and increase the popularity of Ethereum. Afterward, some unidentified group hacked DAO and claim $50 worth Ether.

Advance Developments

On second July 2016, the network of Ethereum was split in ETH (Ethereum) and ETC (Ethereum Classic). After a particular period, Ethereum debated for reorganized decision making and intentionality extra-protocol and ETC for blockchain law code and immutability. After that, Ethereum users, developers, partners, and miners left the ETC (Ethereum Classic) network on 28th of July 2016. Finally, it was November

2016 when Ethereum debloated blockchain, prevent span attacks and increase DDoS.

Chapter 3 – Effect of Blockchain on Computing

Blockchain computing is the most talked term in the IT industry because it is secure and cost-efficient for everyone. It is important to understand its features, architecture and model:

Features of Blockchain Computing

There are five prominent features of blockchain computing that will help you to understand its efficiency:

On-demand Service

You can use the blockchain to configure and deploy apps without any heavy lifting of information technology. Some vendors offer a template to configure your work because it is based on self-service and service models available on-demand. It will help users to interact with the blockchain and perform different tasks, such as deploying, building, scheduling and management. It will help you to access computing capabilities and help users to bring suppleness to their work for current and future uses.

Resource Pooling

Blockchain will enable you to centralize your IT resources and spread its use to available servers. This can maximize the power of shared computing to distribute the capacity as per your requirements. You can get the advantage of peak-load capacity and utilization efficiency. Allocation of resources will be elastic and you can change it to demand.

Virtualization

It is an important feature of the blockchain because you can create a virtual version of your application topologies and move these topologies across the blockchains and between data centers.

Blockchain can increase the accountability of scalability and use. It will make electronic communication easy with the help of networks and devices. The vendors work to provide access to network, storage, memory and CPU.

Accessibility

Blockchain enables your business to launch applications on different platforms, such as Apple TV, android phones, and laptops. The resources will be accessible and reliable. You can use the blockchain on a tablet in the absence of your office network.

Scalability

Blockchain has the ability to scale up and down without hoarding data. Computing capacity may demand spikes and on-demand scalability is similar to elasticity.

Fundamental Concepts of Blockchain Computing

Blockchain refers to a discrete IT environment designed for remote provisioning and gauges IT resources. This term is designed as a metaphor for the internet and offers to remove access to decentralized IT resources. Initially, the symbol of the blockchain was used as a representation of the internet in a variety of specifications and conventional documentation for web-based architecture. Blockchain environments offer IT resources and supply back-end processing competencies. It is based on internet protocols and technologies. Protocols are standard methods used to promote easy communication in a pre-defined manner.

Management and Security Mechanisms

Blockchain computing may pose privacy concerns because the service provider has an ability to access your data in the blockchain anytime. The blockchain can be altered deliberately or accidently or it can even delete information. Some blockchain providers often share details with third parties for the purpose of security and law and order devoid of the warrant. It is written in their privacy policy and the users have to agree on this policy before using services of the blockchain. You will own the legal ownership of data and you can get physical control of equipment because it is more secure. The end users may not understand the risks and issues involved in the blockchain services because they often click "Accept" without even reading it.

Blockchain Architecture

Systems architecture involves the delivery of blockchain computing with multiple components with each other on the loose coupling mechanism, including messaging queue. The elastic provision involves intelligence in the use of tight coupling or loose coupling to mechanisms.

Blockchain Engineering

It is an application of engineering disciplines to blockchain computing and bring a systematic approach to standardization, commercialization and supremacy in operating, conceiving, maintenance and development. It is a multidisciplinary method surrounding contributions from different areas, such as information, performance, web, security, platform, risk, quality engineering, and software.

Types of Blockchain

Blockchain computing is basically based on resource sharing than handling applications via individual devices and local servers. It will be good to use the internet enabled devices for storage and other services. Blockchain will allow the functions of different apps, such as virtual servers and desktop applications. It is easy to take the advantage of blockchain computing and resource sharing the blockchain computing is based on different deployment models.

Public Blockchain

It is a blockchain hosting service delivered to the network for public use and this model can represent blockchain hosting in a better way. The service providers often render infrastructure and services to various clients. Customers can have control on the location of infrastructure and from a technical viewpoint; there is no different between public and private blockchain structure except the level of security offered for numerous services given to the blockchain subscribers and hosting providers.

It is suitable for the business requirement to manage the load and host Saas-based application and many users can consume it. The operational cost of this model is economical and the deal often provides free services or in the form of a particular license policy. The cost can be shared by all users and the public blockchain is profitable for customers by achieving a financial system of scale. The public can get the advantage of free blockchain and it is "Google".

Private Blockchain

It is internal blockchain and the platform is implemented in the blockchain-based environment that is secure and often safeguarded by the firewall. It remains under the governance of IT section of any corporation. This blockchain allows only authorized users and offers a great control to organizations on data. It is tricky to define constitutes of any private blockchain. It may be difficult to define it according to services and variations. The physical systems are hosted internally and externally and they offer resources from a discrete pool for the private services of the blockchain. Business organizations often require these services for private alarm, assignment, and uptime requirements. Security may be evaded in the private blockchain in case of natural catastrophe and interior data theft.

Hybrid Blockchain

It is an important type of blockchain computing and it can be arranged for two or more servers. You can get the advantage of multiple deployment models. It can cross isolation and overcome limitations of the provider. It can't be categorized into private and public community blockchain. It enables users to increase the capability by assimilation, aggregation, and customization with blockchain package and service. The resources can be managed by external or in-house providers. It can be an adaptation among two platforms to exchange the workloads between public and private blockchains as per your needs.

Non-critical resources, such as development and workload testing can be accommodated in the public blockchain and it may belong to a third-party provider. An e-commerce website may be hosted on a private blockchain and offer security and scalability. It is not a major concern for the site of the brochure and hosted on a public blockchain will be really cheap as compared to the private blockchain. The businesses will be more focused on demand and security of their unique presence and implement an effective strategy. It will make your business focused and their unique presence is often implemented on a hybrid blockchain as an efficient strategy. It is known as blockchain bursting and it can be accessed with the hybrid blockchain.

Organizations often use this model to process big data. The private blockchain encompasses business, sales, and various data. It will initiate different queries on the public blockchain because it is efficient to meet the growing demands. Hybrid has flexibility, scalability, and security. You should learn to deal with network connectivity issues and expenditures because you have to deal with a few challenges while using this.

Community Blockchain
It is a good type of hosting and it helps you to setup mutually shared software for your organization, such as bank and trading organization. It will be a multi-talent setup for several organizations and the community

members often share same performance, privacy along with security concerns. The basic intention of this software is to achieve business objectives and the blockchain can internally manage by the third party provider. The cost will be shared by organizations in the similar community. It is possible to use this computing service to manage, implement and build similar projects. The organizations can understand its potential and they often require this service for their business.

Chapter 4 – Frequently Used Terminologies and their Definitions

If you are taking interest in Ethereum, it is essential to learn the terminologies and their definitions. Here are a few frequently used terms and their definitions.

Đ (Stands for ETH)

D with a stroke is a word used in Icelandic, Middle English, Faroese and Old English. It stands for "ETH". It is frequently used in words like Đapp (decentralized application) or ĐEV. In these words, Đ represents Norse letter "eth". The uppercase Đ "ETH" symbolizes the Dogecoin (cryptocurrency).

Dapp (Decentralized Application)

It is a service operated without a main trusted party. This application enables direct communication, agreements and interaction between resources and end users without any middleman.

DAO

DAO is decentralized autonomous organization. It is a particular type of contract on blockchain that is enforced, automate or codify the working of a company, including expansion, spending, operations, fund-raising, and governance.

Identity

It is a set of cryptographically demonstrable interactions that have property created by a similar person.

Digital Identity

The particular set of cryptographically certifiable transactions signed by similar communal key describe the behavior of digital identity. In numerous scenarios of the real world, it is necessary that arithmetical identities overlap with identities of the real world. Confirming this without any violence is a mysterious problem.

Unique Identity

The particular set of cryptographically certifiable interactions has property that was created by a similar person with added constraints that a person can't have numerous unique identities.

Reputation

Property of a character that other objects believe that character can be either (a) competent at a particular task, or (b) trustworthy to a context, i.e. not to deceive others, even for a short-term profit.

Escrow

If two entities (mutually-untrusting) are involved in business, they may desire to pass funds through a 3rd party (mutually trusted party) and instruct this party to send funds to payees after showing the product delivery evidence. It is essential to decrease the risk of payee or payer committing fraud. Both the 3rd party and construction party is known as escrow.

Deposit

It is a digital property put into a particular contract involving a second party like if particular conditions are unsatisfied, this property will be automatically surrendered and credited to the counterparty as an insurance against conditions, or donated to a charitable fund or destroyed.

Web of Trust

If X highly rated Y and Y highly rated Z, then X is trusting Z. Powerful and complicated mechanism to determine the reliability of a particular individual in particular concepts may theoretically be collected from this standard.

Incentive Compatibility

Incentive-compatibility is a protocol if everyone is following the rules and doing well than trying to cheat, at least lots of people are agreed to cheat together at the similar time.

Collusion

In the scenario of an incentivized protocol, when numerous participants conspire (play) together to game the particular rules to their benefits.

Token System

It involves tradeable fungible virtual good. More officially, a token structure is a databank mapping addresses to figures with property that the key permitted operation is a transfer of N tokens from $X - Y$, with particular conditions that N is non-negative, N is lesser than current balance of X and a document approving the transfer is numerically signed by X. secondary "consumption" and "issuance" operations can exist and transaction fees are collected and instantaneous multi-transfers with numerous parties can be possible. Usual use cases are digital gift cards, company shares, cryptographic tokes in networks, and currencies.

Block

It is a data package that has zero or even more transactions, the hash of parent block (previous) and other data. The total blocks, with each block except for the early "genesis block" encompassing the hash of its previous blocks known as blockchain and have the whole transaction history of the network.

Keep it in mind that some cryptocurrencies (blockchain-based) use a word "ledger" as a substitute of blockchain and these two words are approximately equivalent, though in systems that utilize the ledger term, every block contains a copy of present state (for instance, registrations, partially completed contracts and currency balances) of each account allowing its users to dispose of obsolete historical data.

Dapp

Đapp means decentralized application. It is pronounced as Ethapp because of the utilization of uppercase ETH letter Đ.

Address

An address of Ethereum represents one account. For EOA, it is derived as last 20 bytes of the communal key controlling an account, such as cd2a3d9f938e13cd947ec05abc7fe734df8dd826.

The hexadecimal format is based on 16 notation. It is indicated openly by affixing 0x to an address. Console function and web3.js accept addresses without or with this prefix, but their use is encouraged for transparency. Since 2 hex characters represent every byte of address and a preceded address contain 42 characters. Several APIs and apps are meant to implement new address scheme (checksum-enabled) in Ethereum Mist wallet as of 0.5.0.

Hexadecimal

It is a common representation layout for byte sequencing. It is beneficial because the values are epitomized in a particularly compact layout with the use of two characters in each byte (the characters are [0-9] [a-f]).

Ether

It is the name of Ethereum (a currency). This short name is used for computation within EVM. Obscurely, ether is a unit in this system.

EOA (Externally Owned Account)

It is an account controlled by one private key. If you have a private key linked with EOA, you can get the ability to send messages and ether from it. All contract accounts have a particular address. Contract accounts and EOAs may combine in a single type of account during Serenity.

Gas

It is the name of cryptofuel consumed while execitomh codes via EVM. The gas is a payment of performance fee for operation on Ethereum blockchain.

Gas Limit

The gas limit is useable for individual transactions and blocks (block-gas-limit). For each transaction, the gas boundary signifies the determined gas amount that you want to pay for the execution of the transaction. It is designed for the protection of users from getting exhausted while executing malicious or buggy contracts. The floor of gas limit increases with the introduction of the homestead from 3,141,592 gas – 4,712,388 gas (it is 50% increase).

Gas Price

The cost in the ether of a gas unit is specified in a transaction. After launching homestead, the default price of gas decrease from 50 Shannon – 20 Shannon (it is 60% decrease).

Web3

A Web3 paradigm is an important form that refers to a particular occurrence of improved connectedness between decentralization of applications, services, and all types of devices, semantic storage for online information and artificial intelligence apps for the web.

Epoch

It is an interval between every renewal of DAG utilized as seed by PoW algorithm Ethash. The epoch is defined as 30,000 blocks.

Cryptography (elliptic curve)

It refers to a particular approach to public-key cryptography on an algebraic arrangement of elliptic arcs over finite fields.

Wallet

In a generic sense, a wallet is anything that allows you to store ether or other tokens of crypto. In a crypto space, the wallet can be anything from an individual public/private key pair, such as single paper wallet to manage numerous key pairs like Ethereum Mist Wallet.

Contract

A piece of code on Ethereum blockchain to encompass executable functions and a data set. These functions implement with each Ethereum transaction for particular parameters. The input parameters decide the execution of functions and interaction with data within and other than a contract.

Mining

It is a process to verify contract execution and transaction on Ethereum blockchain in an altercation for an incentive in the ether with the help of mining of each block.

Mining Pool

Pooling of available resources by miners, who share processing power on a network and split reward equally, as per the amount of contribution to solving each block.

Mining Reward

The total amount of ether (cryptographic tokens) that is offered to the miner who mined a novel block.

Tate

It refers to a snapshot of data and balances at a specific point in time on the blockchain. It refers to the condition of a specific block.

Blockchain

It is an ever-growing series of blocks of data that grows with each new transaction. Every new block becomes the part of blockchain and chained to current blockchain through a cryptographic proof of work.

Business Terms

Here are a fee business terms that will help you to understand the difference between Ethereum and traditional terms.

Traditional Agreement (Deed Of Partnership)

It is a legal document important to write at the time of formation of a partnership to detail the rights and duties, profit share and important terms and conditions for each partner entering in the partnership venture. It is important to have a deed of partnership in order to avoid potential conflicts in future. It enables you to specify the division of profit between all partners according to their share. It is a legal agreement that helps you to avoid any disputes and differences in future. Deed of partnership should be signed by all partners and stamped by the concerned authorities of your state.

Flight Capital

Funds that are transferred to other countries in order to avoid high taxes or to fulfill the needs of a person are known as flight capital. It is a situation in which investors move their securities to other countries to avoid specific risks, unstable economy or political condition. Sometimes funds are transferred to other countries to get a higher return in the other country. Flight capital is common in those countries that have high inflation rate and offer a low return on the investment because of some certain economic conditions. Flight capital crops up when the assets and money quickly flow out of the country because of the unstable economy of the country.

Deficit Financing

When government expands more money than its revenues (collected through taxes) over an exacting period of time, this situation is known a deficit financing. Borrowing or minting of new funds is necessary during this process to cope with the difference of spending and revenue. Deficit financing shows the inefficiency of government, tax evasion activities and wasteful spending instead of devising countercyclical policy. There can be different reasons for deficit financing, but the influence of government deficit can be great on the national economy. Governments plan this expenditure in order to increase business activities to cover the shortfall by generating additional revenue.

Demerit Goods

Oversupplied goods in the society by the market are known as demerit goods. These goods are harmful to society because of their negative consumption externalities. Use of demerit goods may cause brim over effects on the third party without any compensation. An externality is a condition in which actions of consumers or producers can be the reason for negative or positive effects on the third party. Tobacco, alcohol, drugs, junk food, and prostitution are some examples of demerit goods. It is important to remove the leftover demerit goods from the market otherwise their excessive consumption can put negative effects on the health of consumers and society.

Depression

Depression is a stern and protracted recession in the economic activities. Depression is another name of severe downturn that usually lasts for two or more than two years. A considerable increase in unemployment, diminishing the value of the available currency, diminishing output, frequent rates of bankruptcies and sovereign debt defaults, reduction in trading activities and volatility in the value of currency are some characteristics of depression. Depression can lead to economy shutter down due to a decrease in investments and consumer confidence. Although, the recession is quite normal during a business cycle for few months depression can shut down all economic activities for a number of years.

Direct Marketing

Direct marketing is direct communication with a potential customer through the physical promotional material to convey important information about specific products and services. It does not involve any kind of online marketing or television advertisements. Different promotional materials like catalogs, mailers and flyers are used in direct marketing. It is considered as an effective technique because it removes the "middle man" for the promotion purpose and you can directly convey your message to potential customers. Direct marketing is a preferred way for those companies who do not have brand recognition and also could not afford other marketing techniques because of their smaller advertising budget.

Discount Loan

It is a type of loan that is issued at the desire of borrower and interests as well as other charges are calculated at the time of loan granting. Total of interest and other charges are calculated to deduct them from the face value of the discounted loan. In this type of loan, the borrower gets low amount as compared to the face value but he/she is still responsible to repay the full face value of the loan. The discount loan is a short-term loan and the borrower has to repay complete amount according to the given payment scheduled in installments. The borrower has to pay principal amount on an immediate basis.

Discretionary Order

It is an order that enables broker to delay the execution of a transaction at its prudence with an aim to get a better price for the customer. Discretionary orders are also known as not-held orders, and under these orders, the broker can take the decision about the sale and purchase of securities at best possible price to provide added benefits to customers. Some discretionary orders are restricted in terms to limit the amount of discretion for the broker. Discretion order is used to increase the price range, and the investor is liable to limit the discretion to the broker. A trader can decide the timing of buying and selling of securities.

Double-dip Recession

Double-dip recession is a recession followed by transitory upturn and another recession. It is a situation under which positive gross domestic product growth slithers back to the negative after a specific period of time. Reasons for a double-dip recession may vary in each economy but decelerate trend in the demand for goods and services because of layoffs and expenditure curtails from the previous downturn. Double-dip recession is a worst case for the economy because it can derail the economy and the economy can move back into deeper and long-lasting recession. It can worsen the situation and the recovery of the economy can be really difficult.

Economic Growth

It is an increase in the production capacity of the economy over a period of time. Economic growth is also referred as a rise in the market value of goods and services to yield more. Inflation is a real term that is used to measure the actual economic growth. GDP or GNP per capita is important to consider for the comparison of the economic growth of two countries. Technological changes have great role in the economic growth because the use of latest technology can increase the production rate in a short period of time. It is really easy now to spread the words about your precuts through the internet to grab maximum customers for your business.

Economies Of Scale

It is a cost benefit that rises with the rise in the yield of a product. Contrary association between quantity produced and per unit fixed cost can be the reason for the rise in economies of scale. Fixed cost shared over the production of a large number of goods can reduce the production cost and increase the number of goods produced. It is a better way to reduce per unit variable cost to provide direct benefits to the company. Economies of scale can affect different areas of a large enterprise including production and purchasing department. It can put positive impacts on finances of the organization.

Elasticity Of Demand

Calculation of association between the demand of a good and change in its price over a specific period of time is known as the elasticity of demand. It is an economic term that is used to define price sensitivity and its effects on the demand for a certain product. The elasticity of demand can be calculated as:

Elasticity of Demand = % Change in Quantity demanded / % Change in Price

Any small change in the price can affect the demand and responsiveness of particular products. A large change in price can decrease the demand for a specific product while any smaller change can cause a dramatic increase in the demand for the similar product.

Equilibrium Price

It is a balanced state in which market supply and demand comes at equal level leads to the stability of prices. Typically, excessive supply of certain products in the market can decrease the value of product and decrease in price will increase the demand for the same product. Balance demand and supply of the product brings state of equilibrium. Equilibrium prices indicate a situation in which supply and demands match with each other in balanced proportion. Period of consolidation or oblique impetus can bring supply and demand at equal level and this situation is known as the state of equilibrium.

Exchange Rate

It is a difference between the values of two currencies of two different countries. It is a price of one currency in comparison to the currency of another country. In simple words, the exchange rate is a rate at which you can exchange your currency for the money of another country. The exchange rate can increase or decrease the value of the currency. For instance, the exchange rate of one euro is higher than one yen, and this situation can lower down the value of the yen in another country. Currencies such as Japanese Yen, British Pound and Euro are typically compared with U.S. dollars.

External Debt

Borrowing from foreign lenders for your country is known as external debt. Commercial banks, governments, and intercontinental monetary institutions are foreign lenders. Repayment of loans and interest will be made in the similar currency in which the loan was received. For instance, loan received in US Dollars will be repaid in the same currency.

In order to get required currency, borrower's government may increase exports and trading activities with the lender's country. Countries with weak economy may have to face a debt crisis because of their inability to repay external debt. It shows the inability of borrower's country to generate sufficient profit over a period of time.

Factory Price

In simple words, it is a price charged by a factory for the delivery of goods. It may be the amount of money that is required to purchase important items for the factory including gasoline, machinery, raw material etc. This term refers to the cost of goods at factory other than shipping costs and taxes. Factory price is a price that is quoted by the manufacturer for the pickup of goods from the gate of the factory. Shipping and other costs are not incorporated in the factory price. This price is charged by factory owners in order to generate some additional revenue.

Fast Moving Consumer Goods

These are rapidly sold goods at a comparatively low cost, therefore, these are also known as consumer packaged goods (CPG). Goods like soft drinks, grocery items, toiletries and other perishable items fall under the category of quickly moving consumer goods. The retailers can sell these goods in large amounts by keeping low-profit share.

Walmart, Metro Group, Johnson and Johnson, Colgate-Palmolive etc. are famous retailers of quickly moving consumer goods. These all are globally recognized companies with the largest share in the worldwide market. Fast moving consumer goods are typically low price items like cell phones, digital cameras, mp3 players, video games etc.

Financial Equity

Shares and other financial instruments of an enterprise are usually sold in the share market to increase capital and this process is known as the generation of financial equity. Financial equity raises the funds for business to perform different profitable operations.

Financial securities include IPOs "Initial Public Offerings", preferred stock, quasi-equity instruments, convertible preferred stock, shares, and warrants. These all instruments are treated as financial equity and can be sold to increase the capital of the business. Sale and purchase of financial equity are known as equity financing to fulfill financial needs of the company without taking a loan.

Fiscal Policy

It is an important government policy for the appropriate utilization of government revenue (taxation) and expenditure to bring considerable positive changes in the economy. This policy has great importance because it is used to control unemployment rate, inflation rate and to stabilize business cycle to bring stability to the economy.

Fiscal policy works on the idea of John Maynard Keynes, who thought that the governments have the ability to bring improvements in the bad condition of the economy by adjusting tax rates according to the expenditures of the government. The right application of fiscal policy can bring dramatic improvements in economic conditions.

Fixed Term Contract

It is a contract that is valid for an agreed period of time. An employment contract is an example of the fixed term contract. Under fixed term contract, an employee is responsible to perform his duties up to a particular period of time. Fixed term contract can be made for the completion of certain event or task. Employees under this contract can enjoy similar benefits over a fixed period of time just like permanent employees.

Fixed term contract worker is entitled to the same rights but for short period of time. The contract is designed to explain employment tenure, duties and responsibilities of employee and remuneration details.

Chapter 5 – Effect of Blockchain and Ethereum on Economy

There are a few components of blockchain computing, such as clients, services, applications, platforms, storage and infrastructure.

Services Provided by Blockchain

SaaS (Software as a particular Service)

It is an important model to back web services along with SOA (service-based architecture). It is good for new developing approaches like Ajax. There are different SaaS service offering services via the internet, such as email, CRM, office suite, etc. it is hosted on a scalable infrastructure and can be accessed by an ordinary web browser.

PaaS (Platform as a Particular Service)

It is an integrated and abstracted service to support management, running and development of other applications. It is helpful for developers to scale their apps without worrying for infrastructure.

IaaS (Infrastructure as a Particular Service)

It is a way to deliver servers, storage, space, memory, infrastructure and bandwidth with the self-service console without the help of an IT team.

HaaS (Hardware as Service)

The user can lease the hardware for his personal use and this option enables you to save money on the maintenance of equipment. It can be deployed on your own infrastructure and appropriate software.

Practical Applications of Blockchain Computing

There are a few practical applications of the blockchain computing in the business organizations and different fields:

Blockchain Computing in Business

It offers better hardware, software and network resources to provide unique services on the web and servers. It can identify and meet the logical demands of business organizations and offer innovative services. Organizations currently use traditional infrastructure and enable users to increase the benefits of IT resources in data centers. Companies get the advantage of the traditional management of data centers and practice the use of IT resources for an end user. It can be done in various steps, such as procuring, finding floor space and offer sufficient cooling and power systems. A blockchain can make it easy to implement the automation, workflow of business and abstraction of resources. You can add a shopping card on the website for the convenience of users. This process can increase the efficiency of resources and more than one person can use it at one time.

Blockchain Computing and Education

It is important for educational institutions to quickly respond to the needs of students. They can cope with the fixed budgets and staff. Any challenge in the field of education can be easily handled with the help of blockchain computing. With the help of blockchain computing, education services are reliable and economical in the fast-growing industries of this world. It is good for research, collaboration and discussion. It enables you to run classes at different remote locations and institutes.

Online Entertainment

Lots of people come on the internet for entertainment and these people can get the advantage of blockchain computing. The entertainment based on the blockchain can easily access TV, mobile, set-top box and other forms.

You can get the advantage of the quality of time and better clarity. You can search for (ODE) on demand entertainment, such as news, games, videos, and audio. Amazon, Netflix, YouTube, and Hulu are internet giants and they are earning good profits into the entertainment industry. You can solve ODE puzzles and offer a solution to different issues regarding entertainment.

Blockchain Computing and Telecommunication

Numerous telecommunication companies use blockchaining computing for public and private networks for domestic and commercial purposes. Blockchain communications are voice communications, database communications, and applications hosted by the third-party other than an organization. These can be accessed via the public internet and these communication services help you to manage better relations. You can use a smart phone, tablets, and other third party devices to increase the productivity of your business. These services will be over the support of VoIP system deployments and collaboration for conferencing system. These can be accessed from different locations and you can manage your business with them.

Banking and Finance

With the growth of the international market, there is no need to have a separate database for client and a separate portal for banks. For a faster and advanced business, it is important to offer reliable access to customers to a few major concerns of banks. Financial institutions are quickly using blockchain-based services to increase the agility and reduce the cost of ownership. They offer consolidation, virtualization, data center and storage for easy disaster recovery. The blockchain computing is becoming mature and reliable to increase the adaptation of this system.

Service Provider of Blockchain Computing

There are a few major service providers of blockchain computing to facilitate all customers in a better way:

Google 101-Network

It is based on millions of economical servers that are used to store data, such as numerous copies of World Wide Web. You can search millions of queries at a faster rate.

Microsoft Azure

It is an internet-scale service used as MS data centers and offers a unique functionality to build applications from the web to enterprise scenarios.

Amazon Elastic Blockchain Compute (EC2)

It is a web service interface that offers resizable capacity to blockchain for computing. It is designed for developers to easily use their actual capacity.

IBM BlockchainBrust

It is designed for regular users and it offers blockchain computing service with the IBM blue service software.

Chapter 6 – How to deal with Ethereum and Blockchain?

It is really important to audit your blockchain computing to evaluate data management and security level. There are a few potential risks in blockchain computing:

Access Management Risks
- Provisioning of User's Access
- Access to Super User
- Deprovisioing

Data
- Data separation and segregation
- Privacy requirements
- Information security and information
- Malevolent insider

Financial and Vendor Management

- Penalties or Exit Cost
- Miscalculated start-up costs
- Overhead management
- Variable costs of runaway

Operational

- Service dependability and uptime
- Recovery from Disaster
- Enforcement and SLA customization
- Control on Quality

Regulatory

- Complexity for compliances
- Absence of industrial standards and certifications for the blockchain providers
- Record retention and management
- Lack of visibility in the operations of service provisioning and monitoring for the compliance

Technology

- Sprouting technology
- Cross-vendor integration and compatibility

- Limitation of Customization
- Choices of technology and proprietary impound

Transparency

Blockchain security audit is important to check the security of relevant data to customers. It helps organizations to easily identify the potential risks and threats to develop relevant systems for better security. An employee may grant access to the blockchain from office or home on a business trip. The audit will be good to allow these types of access and avoid others from impersonating justifiable users. A traditional audit requires collection and analysis of date to protect the system from potential threats. Transparency is critical in the security auditing because the relevant data is difficult to obtain as CSP and CSUs.

Encryption

It is risky to store sensitive data outside the home organization and the information will be easy for hackers. In the case of breach of a blockchain, the information will not be secure. It is important for a client to encrypt data in the house before sending it to the blockchain service provider. Traditional infrastructure may face numerous encryption concerns and it is really important for the access to data. If the data pool is encrypted, the organization can efficiently query the data without decrypting it.

Colocation

It is beneficial for multiple organizations to share data and services to the physical system of the organization. It is a cost-reduction method to share technology infrastructure that may lead to greater security concerns. CSPs can be helpful to prevent the system of users from abuse of service and access to client's data. IaaS encounters this problem and turns to hypervisors to insulate the virtual machines. CSP should balance collocation system and hypervisor needs of business for security issues. The combination of a multitude of blockchain-hypervisor and degree of blockchain adoption should include examinations of all CSPs. It is important to assert proper collocation security and a statement will be issued regarding multitenancy without proper segmentation.

Domain to Consider

It is important to consider a right domain on the basis of the data type. A domain-tailored audit will be a right choice for you:

Medical Domain

The medical domain is used by doctors, medical specialists and hospitals. This domain contains sensitive information and it should allow access to pharmacies, auditors, patients and other institutions. The medical domain should be audited because any breach may result in a major loss. The medical domain is a high standard domain and it is important to tailor a perfect audit approach to complying with the legal standards. It should evaluate both medical organization and information. CipherBlockchain can be a good choice for the medical domain.

Banking Domain

Banks may have lots of traffic and the users require various devices to access these services. It is important to keep this information secure and available for all clients who want online access. You have to secure the sensitive data of customers and share information with clients with multiple accounts. Temenos is working to reduce overhead expenses of small banks. It is the responsibility of banks to manage the security of data. The security breach may result in the break of all bank accounts. A traditional audit may store its data at the headquarters of banks. The blockchain infrastructure may pose additional risks and offer unintended access to banking data to competitors.

Government Domain

Governments are also using blockchain domain and it is important to perform CSPs audit to protect sensitive data. For authenticating and authorized an audit of CSPs, the government agencies often use FedRAMP (Federal-Risk-and-Authorization-Management-Program) that is performed for enduring assessment of the service provider.

Three important areas of assessment are changed in the control process, operation visibility and response to incidents. You should submit an automatic data feed to particular agencies for a particular period of time as period evidence for the system performance. Change control process restricts (CSPs) has the ability to change policies and affect the requirement of FedRAMP. You have to deal with possible risks and vulnerabilities because the blockchain system can be a threat to sensitive information.

Evaluate Vendors

It is important to evaluate your vendors for risk and benefits. You should consider the following questions while performing the evaluation:

Relationship with Vendor

It is important to determine the third-party blockchain provider who will work as a liaison between the vendor and company. This will be helpful to ensure their lines of communication and legal department.

Asset Protection Level

You should check the asset protection level and ability to protect the valuable information. It is important to check the security controls in place for the protection of data and intellectual property for the consumer. You can consider SSAE 16s and SAS 70 audit for satisfaction.

Division of Responsibility

Your selected company should have a clear understanding of the security procedures and can monitor and control servers in a better way. You should check their network infrastructure and determine financial and legal responsibility for security and data.

Disaster Recovery Plan

Disaster preparation is really important for business organizations of all types. It is important to check the blockchain computing model to get the advantage of this plan. The company should have disaster recovery plans to determine if they align with recovery objectives and needs of your business.

Multiple Tenants

In a blockchain, your data will be stored on the same machine with other clients and the company should know what to control on logical and physical devices. There should be a separate cage to separate your data from others.

It is important to check technology environment of your blockchain and select a hosting provider that can manage your data in a variety of locations. The company should understand your data needs and control alignment of data with the prospective vendor. You have to perform a gap analysis so that your company can determine any control or process gaps.

Chapter 7 – Security Threats to Blockchain and Ethereum to Avoid any Mishap

Before you understand the security of Ethereum, it is essential to find out the types of attacks exist in the internet world.

The examples of attacks can be classified as passive attacks to monitor communications, active attacks and close-in attacks to exploit the data inside of a system. Some attacks are done through service providers and the information system is an attractive target for the hackers.

Passive Attack

It is an attack to monitor the unencrypted traffic and search for the sensitive information and clear-text passwords. This information is considered useful for other types of attacks. The attacker may analyze the traffic, monitor unprotected communications, decrypt the weak encrypted traffic and collect passwords. Passive interception will prove helpful for adversaries see the upcoming actions and other activities. This action can disclose the data files to other attackers without the knowledge of the user.

Active Attack

In this type of attack, the attacker may bypass a secured system through a virus, stealth, Trojan horses, and worms. These types of attacks are attempted to break the protection features and some malicious codes are introduced to steal or change the information. Active attacks are planned against the backbone of network and information in the passage. During these attacks, the electronic piercing of an enclave, or attack on a remote user while connecting to an enclave are performed. As a result of active attacks, the data files are exposed, DoS or the data is being modified.

Distributed Attacks

In this attack, the codes introduced by the adversary are utilized, such as a Trojan horse or a trusted component of the software that will be distributed to various other users and companies. During distributed attacks, the malicious modifications are done in the hardware and software at the factory or during the distribution. The purpose of these attacks is to introduce the malicious code, like a back door for the products to access them without authorization to get information at a later date.

Close-in Attacks

It is an attempt to get physically close to the components of a network, data, and systems in order to collect maximum information about the network. These may contain regular individuals who are physically close to networks and systems. The attackers try to collect confidential information and modify any data or password to deny access to authorized users to information. Surreptitious entries into the network prove helpful to get physically close proximity and open access.

Social engineering is a famous form of close-in attack because the attacker accesses the information of a particular person through social interaction with him/her. He can send an email message or a phone call. There are numerous tricks that are used to reveal the information about the security of the company.

Insider Attack

In this type of attack, someone is involved from the indoors, such as an unhappy employee. The attack can be both malicious and non-malicious, based on the intentions of attackers. Malicious insiders try to snoop, steal or damage the information. He can use it in fraudulent manners or restrict the access of an authorized user. Negligence, lack of comprehension and deliberate circumvention of protection can't be the reasons behind these tasks.

Phishing Attack

In these types of attacks, the hacker designs a fake website that looks exactly similar to the sites like PayPal or a bank. The hacker then sends an email message to trick users to click a link that leads him/her to the fake side. When the user tries to log on his/her account, their account information is being recorded by the hacker and he/she can try this information on the real website.

Hijack Attack

In this type of attack, the hacker takes over a session between you and your client and disconnects your communication with other individuals. The hacker talks to you just like the other person and you still believe that you are dealing with the original party. You can also send your private messages to hackers.

Buffer Overflow

It is an attack in which the attacker sends maximum data to an application more than its capability of expectations. This time of attacks may result in gaining the administrative access to the system through a command prompt.

Password Attack

In this type of attack, the attacker tries to crack the passwords to get access to your personal information. The database of passwords is their main target and they try to steal them to unlock protected files. There are three major types of password attacks, such as:

- Dictionary attack
- Hybrid attack
- Brute-force attack

In a dictionary attack, a word list is used that can be a list of potential passwords. A brute-force attack is an attempt to combine characters.

Exploit Attack

Exploit attack is a type of attack in which the attacker completely knows the security problems of an operating system and a software. The person can exploit the weak areas to leverage the knowledge.

Spoof Attack

In these types of attacks, the hackers modify a source address of the packets that a person is sending. The receiver considers them as these are coming from someone else. It is an attempt to sidestep your firewall rules.

Routers, firewalls, and switches are primary components of the network. These are gatekeepers for a network to guard your servers and applications against hackers and intruders. Some top level threats of the network are:

- Information Gathering
- Sniffing
- Denial of Service
- Spoofing
- Session Hijacking

Host Threats and Their Countermeasures

Host threats are dangerous for your system software and applications. The Server of Microsoft Windows 2003, Internet Information Services (IIS), Windows 2000 and.NET Framework are important to protect from host threats. Top level host threats are as under:

- Viruses, Trojan horses, and worms
- Profiling
- Password breaking or creaking
- Refutation of service
- Random/arbitrary code execution
- Unauthorized access
- Footprinting

Viruses, Worms, and Trojan Horses

The virus, worm, and Trojan horses are malicious programs that can disrupt your operating system and applications. These threats can attack the applications and operating systems.

Viruses, worms, and Trojan horses can attack through weak defaults, software bugs, errors of users and inherent vulnerabilities in the internet protocols.

Countermeasures
- Stay up-to-date with latest operating systems and software programs.
- Block unnecessary access to all ports at the firewall and host.
- It is important to disable idle functionality, such as protocols and services.
- Change the weak and default configuration settings to make it secure and free from all threats.

Food Printing
It is a famous technique to gather data from a computer system through DNS queries, ping sweeps, port scanning and World Wide Web spidering.

A hacker can get access to your all information by starting with your basic details, such as names, email addresses, etc. They can track your IP address of your website and check online servers.

Countermeasures

You can avoid this by restricting the responses and requested. Make sure to disable unnecessary protocols and evaluate the information before publishing on the website.

In short, if you want to make your system secure from all security threats, it is important to uninstall all unnecessary programs, disable additional protocols, always use strong passwords, recheck the URL of websites before entering your confidential details and hardens the TCP and IP stack against denial of services. You should configure the IIS to reject URLs with "../" because it will help you to avoid arbitrary code execution. Always configure secure web permissions and lock down files and folders with the help of restricted NTFS permissions. Use .NET Framework access control mechanism.

BruteForce Attack

A code word can be cracked with the use of Brute-force attack, and it is a method in which possible amalgamation of numbers, special characters and letters are used. The duration of attacks may vary on the basis of the complexity of the password.

Countermeasure

If you want to avoid this attack, you can avoid long and complex passwords, and try the combination of upper and lower cases and numbers. It may take thousands of years to crack a complex and long password. For instance, a password like "ieatfood" is easy to crack, where a password like "aP85KL31" is difficult to crack.

Social Engineering

Social engineering enables you to manipulate a person to trust you so that you can get information from them.

Example 14

A hacker may try to get the password of a co-worker or friend by calling him/her as an expert of IT department and ask for the login details. The hackers may call the victim pretending to be an officer of the bank and ask for the credit card details. It is used to get a password, bank credentials, and personal information.

Countermcasures

If a person called you as a bank officer and ask for the personal or bank details, then ask them a few questions. Make sure to authenticate the distinctiveness of a person and doesn't give any detail like credit cards, private details or cellular phone numbers on a phone call.

Rats and Keyloggers

In keylogging or rating, a hacker sends keyloggers or rats to the victim. This gives access to the hacker to monitor everything on the computer of a victim. Every stroke is logged, such as passwords and bank details. The hacker can control the computer of a victim.

Countermeasures

If you want to avoid rats or keylogging, there is no need to log in your bank account from a cyber café or the computer of another person. If it is important to use a virtual keyboard, then use an anti-virus software and update them on a regular basis.

Phishing

It is one of the easiest and popular methods of hacking used by hackers to get account details of a person. In these attacks, the hackers make fake pages of the real websites just like Facebook, Gmail, etc. When a person login through the fake page, the hacker can steal the details and use on the real web pages. It is really easy to design fake pages with the help of free web-hosting sites.

Countermeasures

You can easily avoid phishing attacks by checking the URL because the URL of phishing sites is different from original one.

Example 15: URL of the phishing facebook may look like faccbook.com. There can be one different character as you can notice "c" instead of "e" in the URL. Make sure to check the URL and if it is correct, then enter your personal details.

Rainbow Table

Rainbow table is a pre-computed list of hashes and other possible combination of characters. A password hash is processed through a mathematical algorithm like md5 can be transformed into a new thing that can't be recognized. Hash is a way to encrypt the password and after hashing a password, there is no method to get the original string. MD5 is a commonly used hashing algorithm to store the password in the database of the website. It is quite similar to dictionary attack with only one difference that the rain tables attack only hashed characters that are used in the passwords. On the other hand, the dictionary attacks normal characters used in the password.

 "iloveu" in md5 is edbd0effac3fcc98e725920a512881e0 and for hello, it is 5d41402abc4b2a76b9719d911017c592.

Countermeasures
Make sure to select long and complex password because it takes lots of time and resources to create a table for long and complex passwords.

Guessing
It is a silly method, but you can use it because sometimes, it may help to get a password in a few seconds.

It can be done by a hacker who know you and have information about your password patterns.

He can guess the combination or can use social engineering to get the password.

Countermeasures

There is no need to use your own name, phone number, surname, date of birth or any roll number as a password. You can create a password that should not relate to you. Make sure to create a complex and long password with the combination of numbers and letters.

Identify or Cookie Theft and Countermeasures

Personal information can be stolen from your system with the help of cookies. Whenever, you browse a website, a cookie on this website automatically stored in your computer. The hackers can steal this cookie to access your system easily and steal confidential information.

If you browse a website, a cookie is automatically saved in your system so that your information can be easily retrieved from this website on your second visit.

Countermeasure

If you want to protect your system from a cookie or identity theft, then it is important to keep your computer and smartphones clean. Install a good antivirus program like free AVG or Avast and run a full system scan. Keep your antivirus updated to get rid of regular security threats.

STRIDE Threats and Counter Measures

STRIDE threats are faced by applications because the hackers attack your computer in order to steal important details. STRIDE basically stands for:

Spoofing

It is an attempt to access the system with the help of a wrong identity. The hacker often steals the credentials or use a fake IP address. After getting the access as a legitimate user, the hacker abuses the privileges and access personal details.

Countermeasures

Always use strong authentication and avoid storing secret passwords in plaintext form. There is no need to pass your passwords on a wire. Protect authentication cookies with the use of secure sockets layer (SSL).

Tampering

Tampering is an illicit modification of data, for instance, data flower on a network between two computers.

Unprotected data packets can be interrupted and modified. Execution of malicious codes can corrupt the data.

Countermeasures

You can avoid this by using data with hashing and signing. Digital signatures can be used and enhance the strength of your authorization. You can use tamper-resistant protocols crossways communication links.

Repudiation

It is an ability of users to deny the performance of a specific transaction of action. You can't prove these attacks without auditing.

There is a web application that can design access control and authorization on the basis of "JSESSIONID". The action of a registered user will be based on the parameter of users and defined by a cookie header.

Countermeasures

To avoid this attack, you can create secure audit trails and use digital signatures.

Information Disclosure

It is an unwanted exposure of personal data and it can be due to poor handling of data or insufficient security measures.

A user views the content of a file or a table, or a person is not authorized to open or monitor the data, data conceded in plain text on the network.

It can be a use of hidden files, embedded comments, strings in database connection and weak handling of data. It can increase both internal and external threats and your information can be revealed to your opponents. This information can be really useful for a person to avoid hacking attack.

Denial of Service

It is a process to make a system or application unavailable.

A denial of service can be achieved by bombarding requests to servers with the use of all available system resources. The input data can also be malformed to crash the process of an application.

Countermeasures

Resource and bandwidth throttling techniques are good to avoid denial of service attacks. You can use validate and filter inputs to get rid of this problem.

Elevation of Privilege

Elevation of privilege means a user with limited dispensation may assume the identity of a privileged user to access an application and get maximum gains.

An attacker with limited dispensation may increase the privilege level for conciliation and gain the control of highly privileged and trusted account or a procedure.

Countermeasures

You should follow the principles of least dispensation and use least dispensation service accounts to execute the process and access available resources.

Chapter 8 – How Ethereum impact in cryptocurrency and the blockchain technology?

Ethereum is commonly associated with blockchain technology and Bitcoin. It has numerous other apps that allow you to move beyond digital currencies. Building applications of blockchain need a complicated background in mathematics, cryptography, and coding. Formerly unimagined apps from the digitally recorded property and electronic voting to trading and regulatory compliances are actively being deployed and developed faster than before. By offering tools to developers to build decentralized apps, Ethereum is resolving all possible issues.

Ethereum platform allows developers to build decentralized applications. Just like Bitcoin, new Ethereum is a public distributed blockchain network. Though there are numerous technical differences between Bitcoin and Ethereum, it is essential to note that the Ethereum and Bitcoin differ substantially in capability and purpose. Bitcoin offers a specific application of a P2P electronic cash system to activate online payments of Bitcoin. While blockchain Bitcoin is useful to track ownership of bitcoins (digital currency), the blockchain Ethereum focuses on running programming codes for decentralized applications.

The miners in Ethereum blockchain work to get Ether instead of mining for another currency bitcoin. Ether is a crypto token used to fuel the network. Outside a tradeable cryptocurrency, Ether is used by app developers to pay for services and transaction fees on Ethereum network. Ethereum is potentially overtaking Bitcoin in the digital currency's market. Currency is virtual in every economy. Bitcoin is a leading coin and the price of other coins are measured by the value of Bitcoin.

Ethereum is different in technology and it is another cryptocurrency. Value of ethereum coin is known as Ether and similar to Bitcoin, it is sold and bought and utilized by investors to buy ICO opportunities. The main difference between Bitcoin and Ethereum is a fact that Bitcoin is only a currency, but the Ethereum is a particular ledger technology that is used to develop new programs. Both Ethereum and Bitcoin operate on blockchain technology, but the Ethereum is better and robust. If the Bitcoin was 1.0 version, then Ethereum is version 2.0. It proves helpful in the building of decentralized apps.

In short, it is an excellent tool for innovations. Moreover, Ethereum technology has heavy support as Enterprise Ethereum Association. This is one of the Fortune 500 organizations that are agreed to work together to build band learn blockchain Ethereum technology. These are often known as smart contract technology. Smart contracts display that demanding business apps can automate complex applications. The Ethereum allows you to create apps across a broad range of industries and services. Developers are in uncertainty so it is difficult to know successful apps and failed experiments. Here are some projects.

Weifund: It offers a platform for numerous crowdfunding campaigns and leverages smart contracts. It allows contributors to turn into contractually sponsored digital assets sold, used or traded within the ecosystem of Ethereum.

BlockApps: This platform wants to provide an easy path for enterprises to deploy, manage and build blockchain apps. From the evidence of concept to full production integrations and systems with bequest systems. It offers all important tools to create public industry-specific, semi-private and private blockchain applications.

Uport: It offers a secure and convenient way for users to have maximum control over their personal information and identity for third parties. Instead of trusting on government organizations and compromising their identities to 3rd parties. Users can control the people who may access and utilize their personal information and data.

Provenance: This platform is utilizing Ethereum to turn misty supply chains transparent. By tracing histories and origins of products, this project objects to create an accessible and open framework of data so that the consumer can make right decisions while buying products.

Augur: It is an open-source forecasting and prediction market platform. This platform allows everyone to predict events and earn rewards for their right predictions. Predictions on the future events of the world, such as the winner of the next elections of the United States. People can earn monetary rewards after right predictions.

Chapter 9 – Understand the Mining Procedure for Ethereum

Mining is an intensive work that involves lots of computation that needs plenty of time and processing power. Mining is an act of contributing in disseminated cryptocurrency system in consensus. The miner gets rewards for offering solution to the challenges of math problems. It needs a computer hardware to utilize with mining apps.

Whole information on the transactions of cryptocurrency should be embedded in data blocks. Every block is associated internally with numerous other blocks. This generates the blockchain and these blocks should be analyzed as soon as possible to confirm smooth running and operations of transactions on a platform.

Although the issuers of these currencies don't have the particular processing capabilities to manage this alone. It is the place where miners are needed.

A miner works as an investor who devotes time, energy and computer space to sort through blocks. When a mining procedure hits the accurate harsh, they can succumb their solutions to issuers. After proper verification, the issuer of a currency offer rewards that can be a portion of the similar transaction they assisted in verifying. They may obtain digital coins in exchange for mining work. The outcomes of mining (digital mining procedure) are known as a POW (proof of work) system. A few currencies depend only on this system, while others are using a blend of POW (proof of work) and POS (proof of stake).

The word mining originated from the analogy of gold of cryptocurrency domain. It is not a scheme for someone to easily get rich, but it needs effort and time to grow while working alone. This special word was embraced because only precious materials are hard to see, and digital currencies are equally precious. Mining should help a miner to increase the volume of valuable metals in the financial market. Digital mining should be executed with the increase in the circulation of digital currencies.

The situation is same for Ethereum. If you want to utilize Ethereum, you have to get the advantage of mining. Although, mining Ethereum means increasing the circulation volume of Ether. It is essential to secure the network of Ethereum because it creates, propagates, publishes and verified blocks in the blockchain. Through Ethereum mining procedure, you can mine Ether. Mining ether is equal to securing a network that ensures certified computation in turn.

Ether is really important because it works as a fuel to smoothly run the platform of Ethereum. Typically, Ether is utilized as an incentive to increase the motivation of developers to develop top-notch apps.

Each developer tries to engage and develop the use of improved smart contracts on blockchain Ethereum. They need Ether for this procedure so it is a cheap fuel for the platform. The miners can sell their Ether after finishing mining. Supply of ether is limited and the total ethers and operations of network decide the presale. Almost 18 million Ethers are issued annually that is almost 25% of the 1st issue. It works as a particular system to decrease inflation.

Every block should possess the POW (proof of work) of the mentioned difficulty to validate in consensus. Validation algorithm is known as Esthash. Uniform output in distribution requires time and involve some complications. Miners can manipulate the difficult to control the time required to search a novel block.

In mining of Ethereum, the difficulty is dynamically adjusted so that network produces a block after every 12 seconds. Synchronization of a system makes this work easy. You can do ethereum mining at your home. It needs some command prompt and script writing knowledge. It is really exciting and easy after breaking it into manageable steps.

Basics of Mining Procedure

Before you learn the steps of Ethereum mining, you should pay attention to some basics:

Ether mining needs lots of electricity. If you can efficiently manage the mining practices, you can generate more income by selling Ether. You can calculate profit with the help of calculators of ethereum mining. There is no need to use an ordinary calculator.

If you have a personal computer with the GPU (Graphic Card) 2 GB of RAM, you can use it to mine Ethereum. CPU (Central Processing Unit) mining is a frustrating exercise. It may take periods to finish and your profit will be really good. GPU can give you the best bet; therefore, you should have 200 times better GPU than CPUs to mine ether. Keep it in mind that AMD cards are better than Nvidia cards. Before you follow the given steps, you have to focus on some important details.

Mining procedure needs plenty of electricity and it can be a problem for you. If you want to earn money, try to carry out this practice efficiently. Here are a few steps to follow for mining procedure. It is essential to free lots of space on the hard drive of your computer. Almost 30 GB can be a good choice for blockchain and any other software.

Mining Procedure of Ethereum

You have to download an app known as Geth. This app will become a communication hub and link you to the digital platform Ethereum while synchronizing your setups, such as hardware and other components. It will report each new development that needs your action.

You may get Geth in a Zip file so unzip it and carefully transfer files to HDD. The drive C can be the best choice to transfer files.

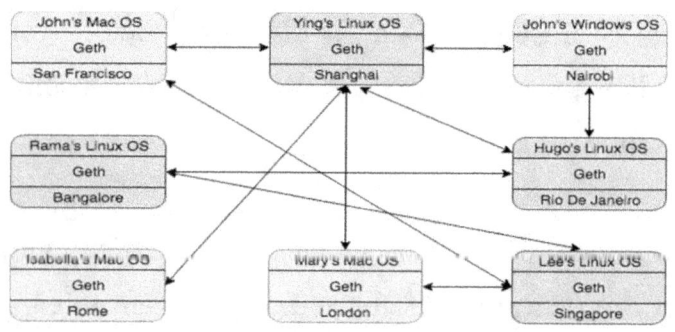

Ethereum Blockchain Network

You have to execute an installed app via command prompt. Search "CMD" in windows, if you don't know about command prompt and click CMD from a search list.

"C:\users\name of user> the name of user placeholder will be the current name of your PC and becomes the typical display format of command terminal. In the next step, locate Geth and type "cd/" in the terminal of command prompt. This instruction will change the directory. "C:\>" must be highlighted now that means you are in C: drive.

Next step will be account creation. You have to make Geth a call and type "geth account new" in the command terminal and enter key. There will be "c:\>geth account new" in the command terminal.

At this stage, you have to set a password and take care of this password. Make sure to remember your password and for this purpose, you can write it in your diary or phone. Carefully type this password and enter again after typing this password and congratulation, your account is generated.

You have to link Geth with a particular network before making other things operational. Write in "geth –rpc" in the terminal and hit enter. This action initiates the download of blockchain Ethereum and harmonizes with a global network.

This procedure is time-consuming and depends on the current size of the blockchain and speed of internet connection. You have to patiently wait for the completion of this procedure before mining.

To proceed at this stage, you should have a special mining software that allows a GPU to run the hash algorithm for the platform. You can download Ethminer to lift this heavy procedure.

Install a mining software like Ethminer or any other software of your choice to complete this procedure.

Replicate 4th step after opening a new command terminal (change command of the directory). If you want to open another command terminal, just right-click on the past icon of the active terminal in your taskbar and hit on this terminal for the menu.

Type "cd prog" in a new terminal command window followed by a tab key. There will be "C:\>cd prog" on the display. Carefully hit tab key once again and see the display 'C:\>cd "program files"' and push enter key to see 'C:\program Files>.'

If you want to go in the software folder of Ethereum mining, you have to write 'cd cpp' and hit tab and enter keys. You have to hit tab again and the terminal will display 'C:\Program Files\cpp-ethereum>.'

If you want to start mining with a GPU, you should key in ethminer –G followed by an enter key. This procedure will start the mining procedure after developing (Directed Acyclic Graph) DAG that is a larger file stored in your RAM of GPU to make its Application Specific Integrated Circuits (ASIC) resistance. Make sure to have enough space on your drive before starting this procedure.

Similarly, if you are up for the procedure, CPU mining will be an easy task. Just write "Ethminer" and press enter key to initiate this procedure. This DAG building needs you to do this step to let Geth take over whole communication with an app Ethminer.

Future Scope of Ethereum

Presently, Ethereum utilizes PoW (proof of work) system and working as an arm supporting for blockchain technologies, such as Ethereum and bitcoin. PoW refers to the solution of complex equations that is the main requirement for the miners to clear for their blocks before adding them to blockchain technology. This system is separated because of electricity cost and environmental damage caused by it. Although the use of Dagger Hashimoto algorithm can be beneficial because it allows Ethereum to generated a path to permit home computers to efficiently mine with little and necessary expenditure.

Moreover, Ethereum is really calm for its next update, to take out the mining concept and replace it with a new proof of taking mechanism. This mechanism will get power through a consensus algorithm.

The network of Ethereum is an elongated string of connections managed by computers and their influence is undeniable and the profit obtained from mined Ether is weird. People thought that the mining may be topped with the advancement of consensus algorithm. It can be a good time to mine for curious people.

Chapter 10 – Investment, Trading, Buying and Selling in Ethereum

Purchase of Ethereum can be an easy procedure via Ethereum exchanges. After purchasing Ether for a fiat currency like GBP, EUR or USD, the funds will be stored on exchanges or personal secure wallet. For small ethereum purchases, users can store their crypto on exchange for their convenience. Large purchasers should move their funds in a secure wallet. Moreover, investors may trade Ethereum without buying and securing this currency through CFD platform like eToro.

Registered Ethereum Exchanges

If you want to purchase Ethereum, you can choose an exchange and register your account, deposit Euros or US dollars and purchase Ethers. The followings are a few Ethereum exchanges.

eToro

This platform offers CFD trading that allows users to easily trade the cost of Ethereum without securing and purchasing this cryptoasset. It is a social platform for investment for the traders of Europe. This company is more interested in cryptocurrency trading. The minimum purchase limit is $200 and this platform is friendly for beginners. You can buy via PayPal, bank transfer or debit/credit card. This platform is regulated and authorized by FCA (Financial Conduct Authority of UK).

Coinbase

If you want to trade in Ethereum, the coinbase is another famous platform. This exchange is available in numerous countries of Europe, USA and United Kingdom. Residents of Australia can purchase Ether at this exchange, but they should use another exchange to sell AUD cryptoasset. The minimum purchase limit is $1 and you can buy with banks, debit/credit cards. Again this exchange is good for beginners.

Plus500

The minimum purchase of this exchange is $100 and you can buy with PayPal, Bank, credit and debit cards. This CFD trading platform is friendly for the beginners to trade cryptocurrencies.

Localethereum

This exchange is anonymous for sellers and buyers of Ether. It is powered by smart contracts and is a new place to purchase Ether. The minimum purchase limit is $1 and you can purchase with cash, any other cryptocurrency, PayPal, and bank. This platform is not good for beginners.

Other Exchanges to Buy and Sell Ethereum

BitPanda and Bitstamp are two other platforms for ethereum trading. Both platforms are good for beginners. You can buy with bank and debit/credit cards. For BitPanda, the minimum purchase limit is $25 and this limit is $5 for Bitstamp.

Kraken, Gemini, and GDAX are three platforms that are not friendly for beginners. You can trade via bank transfer only. The minimum purchase limit of GDAX, Gemini and Kraken are $1, $1 and $5 respectively.

Steps to Buy an Ether

The procedure of Ether purchase may vary at every exchange, though the principles remain same. If you are new to currency, there is no need to worry. Lots of exchanges make this procedure really easy just like transfer of an online payment.

Register at Your Favorite Exchange

There are numerous exchanges in the market; therefore, you have to do some research. Your selected exchange will depend on your governing laws, personal preferences and living style. Register at your selected exchange and complete the procedure by entering your information.

Complete Identity

Before depositing or withdrawal, exchanges should carry out KYC (know your customers) and AML (Anti-money laundering) checks. Exchanges will need your identification photo and proof of address to proceed.

Select a Method for Deposit

Every Ethereum exchange offers its own method of baking. They may offer a mix of PayPal or debit/credit card, SEPA and wire transfer via bank. Every exchange charge a particular fee on every deposit method. Fee details can be checked in the footer of the website of exchange.

Deposit Currency

Deposit may take between 24 hours to numerous days to arrive in your account of exchange. Deposit time can vary in each exchange and method of deposit.

Buy Ether with Deposited Funds

After getting your fiat currency in your exchange account, it is possible to use this currency for the purchase of Ether. Coinbase is a good platform for every beginner.

Ethereum Investment

Ethereum blockchain ledger contains history of each and every transaction. This ledger is secured via a particular network containing machines. Each machine work to validate and process transactions. The currency of Ethereum blockchain is Ether and it is issued with the use of these machines to manage this work. Ether is easy to trade for fiat money, such as Euros and dollars. Thousands of participants are available on this network for transactions without any middleman.

Ethereum transactions will be immutable and final. If a user makes an invalid transaction for any reason, such as lack of funds, then this transaction will not become the part of the blockchain. The whole history of valid transactions is stored by different machines in plenty of physical locations. Each copy is identical to another copy. Distributed nature of Ethereum blockchain make it free from the central point of failure and decrease the possibility of shut down.

Basically, the value of Ethereum blockchain was less than one dollar in 2015 July at the time of its launch. The price of Ethereum slowly climbed until 2017 March when the market of cryptoasset notices a massive surge in the price of Ethereum.

Purchasing Anonymously

Some people prefer P2P route for the purchase of Ethereum to avoid AML and KYC. They purchase large quantities through this route. This act may be sulked by the regulators of the country, so you should do it at your own risk. This route needs you to purchase Bitcoin and exchange them for Ethereum. You have to set up a secure wallet for

Ethereum. If you need a trusted volume, you can visit Ethereum.org.

Reasons to Put Money in Ethereum

There are numerous reasons to put your money in Ethereum, such as:

By purchasing Ethereum as investments, you can access blockchain investments and token sale. It will become easy for you to hedge against the fiat incumbent system. Customers can get a chance to diversify their portfolio.

You can buy Ethereum to use in EVM and smart contracts. These allow you to interact with IoT blockchain-based devices. It will become easy for you to pay salaries internationally.

Investment Strategy for Ethereum

Investment strategies for Ethereum may vary and it is associated with your own risk tolerance. These directions are for information purpose and in case of any doubt, you can consult a reliable financial adviser.

Buy, Hold and Diversify

One of the best investment strategies for a crypto asset is "buy cryptocurrency and hold". If you want to replace Ethereum with a fiat currency to a friction, its value must be greater than the current value. If Ethereum can become the favorite currency for payable web machine that will permit billions of devices to efficiently transact value with each other. The Ethereum volatility allows people to consider the averaging of dollar cost while spending the sum of investment in chunks over a particular period to acquire Ether at a particular price.

Predicting the Ethereum's future is just like predicting the weather in five years. It is improbable that Ethereum may disappear anytime, but Ethereum has shown Bitcoin and it is possible for a cryptoasset to become a dominant force in a limited period. You can purchase Ethereum to exchange for numerous other cryptoassets, such as ETC (Ethereum Classic) and XRP (Ripple) to hedge against the unexpected disappointment of a given coin. Numerous technologists and VCs agreed that particular cryptoassets may become ubiquitous in the future.

Some investors prefer day trading cryptoassets on particular exchanges like GDAZ and Poloniex. This practice can compound risk on a volatile asset and must be treated carefully.

Ethereum Wallets

If you want to easily secure your Ether, you will need a secure Ethereum wallet. Before purchasing your Ether, you should know about wallet software and cryptocurrency transactions. Ethereum is quite similar to any other cryptoasset and a false move while receiving and sending a transaction may result in the loss of the whole bankroll. You can mitigate this risk by having the basic understanding of using technology with caution.

You will definitely need an Ethereum wallet that is a piece of software to store Ether funds. Ethereum wallets may be a hardware/paper wallet, online exchange, web/mobile app and desktop application. You can download official wallet for Ethereum at Ethereum.org.

Light Client Wallet for Ethereums

New users often download "full node". The full nodes may be used as one wallet, however, these wallets require users to download a full blockchain Ethereum. A new user should start with a light client because these don't need full blockchain for operations. Some examples are:

- Jaxx.io (it also supports numerous other cryptoassets)
- MyEtherWallet

Private Key

After selecting an Ethereum wallet, you have to generate a private key for this wallet before depositing your funds. The private key offers you full access to wallet and funds in it. While creating your wallet, you may be asked to copy a private key. You may generate an offline private key and this information will not be sent on the server and can't be intercepted. You are free to backup and store your private key. Some users use cloud storage to secure their private key with offline prints of the private key or 2-factor authentication. If you have larger sums of Ethereum, you should use hardware wallets as extra security measures.

Addresses and Transactions

After downloading your Ethereum wallet and securing your private key, you have to learn about Ethereum transactions. Your wallet will automatically produce some receiving addresses called public keys that can be a function of a private key. Unlike your private key, the addresses may be freely distributed without any theft risk to make payments and add funds to wallet.

All transactions on blockchain Ethereum are visible publicly through Etherscan (a blockexplorer). For instance, see the below transaction with two public keys.

- From:
  0xea674fdde714fd979de3edf0f56aa9716b898ec8
- To:
  0x3d167984ae0868194ffd97759ff74e342ff3140d

With the use of MyEtherWAllet, the transaction can be really simple to the input address to send funds and fee (gas limit). The later will be automatically set via a software, but it should be a double check to avoid miscalculation of cost. The address is selected automatically on the basis of the balance of every address. After sending transactions, the transaction has is developed and displayed to you in this software. The transaction hash may be put into one block explorer and similar details can be noticed for a new transaction.

Block Height & Confirmations

Your transaction will be included in the minced block. It roughly takes 15 seconds to mine one block. The duration between the broadcast of the transaction (sent to one receiving address) to the time when it is included in one block is a period for pending transaction. Inclusion in one block is known as a confirmation. Every mined block is just like another confirmation. The increase in the number of confirmations for a transaction makes it bedded-into a blockchain. A transaction with more than 30 confirmations are considered tremendously secure and they may persist in blockchain for all perpetuity. Block height can be a block number after the creation of blockchain.

Receiving Transactions

A similar idea of sending is applied to receiving Ether. If you want to purchase Ethereum, after buying it from an exchange, the withdrawal function of the exchange will ask for an address of your wallet. You have to input an address along with the amount of your Ether for withdrawal and after confirmation, you will get transaction has. The Ether may immediately display "pending" in the wallet and you have to follow some confirmations while using transaction has on Etherscan.io.

Safety for Ethereum Transaction

If you want to make the Ethereum transactions safe, here are a few guidelines for you:

Copy & Paste Address

Instead of typing your wallet address, you can copy and paste it. Addresses are case-sensitive and long and any mistake may result in you to lose your funds forever. You will not get a customer support number or chargeback in Ethereum.

Carefully See the Transaction Fee

Only a reliable Ethereum wallet can show the calculated fee of the transaction in cents and dollars. Make sure to double check the transaction fee to pay a reasonable amount.

Double Check Your Address

After copying and pasting an address to receive or send Ether, you have to check it, again and again, to ensure that it is absolutely correct. Look at the last and first letters will ensure that you have pasted it correctly. A reliable wallet software can also confirm an address for receiving or sending. This will decrease the risk of any malware intercepting and substituting the address you are inputting.

Test a Transaction

Ethereum adoption may drive you because of its low transaction charges. There is no problem in sending some Ether to test your understanding of this procedure and for verification of details. This is essential to ensure that everything is going well while sending large amounts.

Hardware Wallets

If you want the maximum security of your Ethers, you can generate hardware wallets. These wallets work offline to generate and secure private keys offline. There is no point to expose your private key to a connected device. You can store your coins offline to avoid the risk of digital theft and attack vectors. Other Ethereum wallets offer you recovery seed upon creation a special PIN is selected for the secure access to devices. For the security of wallet, you have to protect recovery seed and PIN because some malicious individual can access them and steal your funds. Moreover, you can choose multi-signature wallets and 2-factor authentication for maximum security of your wallet. Two most reliable wallets are Ledger Nano S and Trezor. You can try these wallets.

In short, you can secure your wallet in different ways and security options will be based on your possible risk tolerance. The above information will serve as inspiration for the security of your wallet. It is essential to focus on the recommendations of your selected wallet for optimum security.

Chapter 11 – PowerShell Script Writing for Ethereum

PowerShell has extensive and console-based assistance and it is similar to the man pages in the Unix shells via cmdlet of Get-Help. Local contents often retrieve from internet through update-help cmdlet. It helps you from the web and you can acquire it on a regular basis through the –online switch for Get-help.

Windows 10 is available with the PowerShell 5.0 and the Windows 8.1 is available with PowerShell 4.0. This latest version hosts various new features and these are designed to make language simple, easy to use, and avoid some common errors. If you want to use early version of this PowerShell on the operating system Windows, you can migrate from to the required version of

PowerShell to increase its benefits. It helps the system administrators to easily manage each and every aspect of Windows. It also offers particular control on Lync-based servers, Exchange and SQL.

You can find out about the PowerShell version with the help of following commands and press Enter:

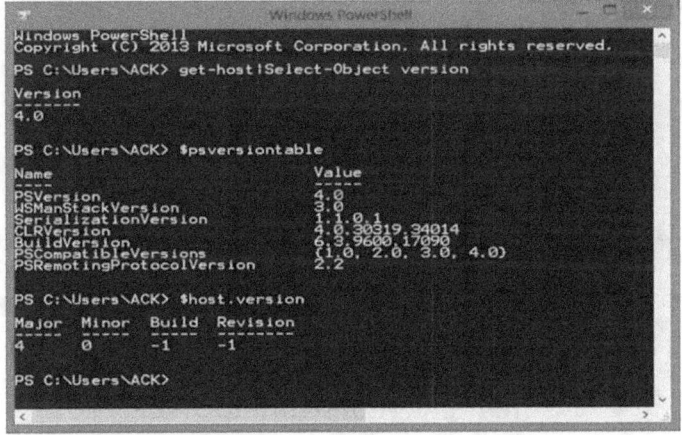

- $psversiontable
- $host.version
- Get-host|Select-Object version

Features of PowerShell

The 3.0 PowerShell is introduced with new functions, such as:

- Workflows of Windows PowerShell
- Cmdlets over-objects (CDXML)
- CIM cmdlets
- Web Access of Windows PowerShell
- Automatic loading Module
- Disconnected and Robust sessions
- Scheduled jobs
- Updatable Help

The features of Windows 4.0 PowerShell are as follows:

- Web Access to the improvements of Windows PowerShell
- Desired-State-Configuration (DSC)

- Windows PowerShell New features Web Services
- Workflow enhancements
- Save-Help

Features of Windows 5.0 PowerShell have the given functionality, such as:

- DSC enhancements
- Classes are defined in the functionality

Major augmentations to repairing, such as the capability to repair the jobs of Windows PowerShell

- Transcriptions are available in hosts
- Module of Network switch
- Manage software packages for OneGet
- Manage the PowerShell of Windows modules PowerShellGet via OneGet
- Enhance performance with the use of COM objects

Windows 5.0 PowerShell is included in the Windows 10 and introduced the given functionality:

PowerShell Workflow of Windows: The capacity brings the actual power of the workflow Foundation of Windows to the PowerShell of

Windows. It is easy to write workflows in the XAML or PowerShell Windows language and run these options similar to the cmdlet.

Improvements in Current Core Cmdlets and the Providers

The PowerShell 3.0 of Windows include unique features for current cmdlets, including the new parameters and the simplified syntax for cmdlets, such as CSV cmdlets and computer cmdlets, Get Command, Getchildltem, Get-History, Get-Content, Securitycmdlets, Measure-Object, Select-String, Tee-Object, Start-Processes, Test-Connection, .Add-Member and Tee-Object.

Discovery and Important of Remote Module

The PowerShell 3.0 of windows extends the module of importing discovery and inherent capabilities on the remote computers.

Cmdlets of the Module

The import modules has capability on the remote computers to your local computer with the use of PowerShell of Windows.

Session Support of New CIM

It offers permission to utilize the WMI and CIM to manage the computers (non-Windows) by importing different commands to your local computer that run indirectly on remote computers.

Auto-Complete Features

These features will help you to save your time and reduce the chances of your typos.

Intellisense PowerShell 3.0

It helps you to underline the errors that you will make in red and get suggested corrections as you hover the pointer of mouse over a curly line.

Update-Help Cmdlet

This will help you to cure various small errors and annoy typos in the integrated documentation.

Improve the Solace Host Experience

With the help of underlying changes, the PowerShell of console host applications can activate in the PowerShell 3.0. The new "Run with the PowerShell" option in the file explorer will help you to run the scripts in one unrestricted session with right-click.

Shared and RunAs Host Support

This RunAs feature is particularly designed for the PowerShell workflow of windows and help users of one session confirmation to create different sessions. These sessions will be run with the approval of one shared user account. This SharedHost new feature helps various users of various computers to easily connect to the workflow session synchronously and track the actual progress of workflow.

Particular Character Handling Enhancements

With one quick lap all the way around the PowerShell 3.0 Windows shows to expand the ability of program to correctly handle and interpret particular characters, LiteralPath parameter that handle particular characters in the paths is valid on all cmdlets with one path parameter, such as Save-Help cmdlets and Update-Help.

The PowerShell of Windows is one Windows command-line shell and it is designed especially for the system administrators. The PowerShell has one interactive prompt and one scripting environment that can be used in combination or independently. Unlike other shells that return and accept text. The PowerShell of windows is often built on the top of .Net FrameWork communal language runtime (CLR) and .NET Framework and returns and accepts the objects of .Net Framework. This important change in environment transports the whole set of new methods and tools to configure and manage windows.

The PowerShell of Windows often introduces the actual concept of the cmdlet and one single function command-line tool in the shell. You can utilize every cmdlet separately and their power can be realized as you use simple tools with complex tasks. The PowerShell of Winodows has more than 100 basic cmdlets and you may write your own cmdlets and share these cmdlets with others.

Similar to various others, the PowerShell of Windows offer access to the file system on your computer. The providers of Windows PowerShell enable you to get access to the data stores, such as certificate stores of digital signature are easy to access with the file system. This guide will help you to learn about Windows PowerShell and cmdlets language, utilization of objects and the providers. You will find the requirements of system there along with particular features, including CIM commands, integrated scripting (ISE) environment and the workflows.

Requirements for Operating System

The 4.0 PowerShell runs on the latest Windows version:

- The Windows 8.1, by default installation.
- 2012 of Windows Server R2, by default installation
- Windows 07 and its 01 service pack, you will install the 4.0 Framework of Windows to run updated PowerShells.
- 2008 Windows Server and R2 with the 01 Service Pack, you have to install 4.0 Management Framework of windows to get latest 4.0 PowerShell.

The 3.0 PowerShell versions are available for the given varieties of Windows:

- By default installation of Windows 8
- 2012 Windows installation

Framework of Microsoft .NET

Requirements

- If you want to use Windows 4.0 PowerShell, you should have a complete installation of the 4.5 .NET Framework of the Microsoft. The windows 8.1 and the 2012 server R2 have 4.5 .NET Framework for Microsoft by default.

- The 3.0 PowerShell of windows requires complete installation of the .NET Framework 04. The Server 2012 and Windows 8 have 4.5 .NET Framework of Windows by default; it should fulfill all important requirements.

- If you want to install the 4.5 .NET Framework of Microsoft (dotNetFx45_Full_setup.exe), you can get this from the download center of Microsoft

- To install the full installation of Microsoft .NET Framework 4 (dotNetFx40_Full_setup.exe). , you can get frame work from the download center of Microsoft.

3.0 Ws-Management

The 3.0 and 4.0 PowerShell of Windows requires 3.0 WS-Management that supports WSMan protocol and WinRM service. This program may be included in the 8.1 Windows and server R2 2012, Server 2012 and Windows 8 and the 4.0 Framework of Windows management and 3.0 Framework of Windows Management.

Instrumentation 3.0

The 3.0 and 4.0 Windows PowerShell requires the proper management of WMI 3.0 instrumentation. You can get this program in 2012 server of Windows and Windows 8.1 or advanced, R2, Server 2012 and Windows 8, the 4.0 Management Framework. You may not be able to access program on your computer, the features may require WMI and the CIM command may not run.

The 3.0 and 4.0 PowerShell of Windows may be complied against the CLR 4.0 (common linguistic runtime).

Graphical User-Interface Requirements

The PowerShell of Windows is based on console applications that may not require any graphical user-interface. It is suitable for the computers without monitors, user interface and screens, such as R2 server 2012 or Windows 2012 server. There are some items that are required for the graphic user interface.

- Incorporated Scripting Environment of Windows PowerShell (ISE)
- Cmdlets
1. Out-GridView
2. Show-Command
3. Show-ControlPanelItem
4. Show-EventLog

Strictures

1. Get-Help cmdlet ShowWindow stricture.

2. Register-PSSessionConfiguration, Set-PSSessionConfiguration cmdlets and ShowSecurityDescriptorUI.

Engine Requirements for Windows PowerShell

It is compatible with the PowerShell 3.0 along with 2.0 versions. The cmdlets providers, modules, scripts and snap-ins written for the 2.0 and 3.0 PowerShell may run without any changes in the windows.

Any alteration in one runtime policy for activation in the Microsoft 04 .NET Framework, the PowerShell Windows hosts programs written for the 2.0 PowerShell and accumulated with CLR (communal language runtime). It is difficult to run it without adjustment in the 3.0 PowerShell for its compatibility with 4.0 CLR.

2.0 contraption of windows PowerShell requires Microsoft .NET (2.0.50727) Framework at minimum. The 1st Service pack and 3.5 .NET Framework of Microsoft has fulfilled this requirement. Unfortunately, the .NET Framework 04 and later releases are unable to fulfill this requirement.

Preinstallation Environment of Windows

The 2.0 and 3.0 PowerShell and 4.0 PowerShell of Windows runs in the Preinstallation Environment and the Windows PE. The following cmdlets may not be maintained:

- Circumstantial Intellectual Transfer Service Cmdlets
- Update-Help
- Save-Help
- WinRM service
- Get-WinEvent
- Get-EventLog

These services are not supported by the Windows PE. You can get the advantage of these applications to create scripts and run them as per your needs. Some Windows have by default PowerShell or you can download from a data center of Microsoft.

How to Write and Run Scripts from the PowerShell Command Line?

It is easy to open and modify the PowerShell of Windows in your Script Pane. This particular file in windows are .ps1 (script files) .sd1 (script-data files and .psm1 (module file of script. These types of files have syntax colored in the pane editor of script. The other types of files are easy to open in the script pane and configure XML, text and .ps1xml files.

Create a Script File

If you want to create one script file, you should click on "New" on the tool bar or the file menu and hit "New". One created file will be appeared in one file tab under the existing tab of PowerShell. You should remember that the tabs of PowerShell are visible only when they are more in number than one. One type script file is created by default and you can save it with new extension and name. Various script files are often created in the similar PowerShell tab.

Open One Existing Script

On your toolbar, you have to hit open or you can also check the file menu and hit open and a dialog box will be there. It is easy to select the type of file you want to open and it will be appeared in the new tab.

If you want to close any file, you can hit the (X) icon on your script tab.

On the tab of file, you can check the name of file and qualify the path of your script files in the tooltip.

You can run script by hitting its icon in the toolbar and click run after selecting file.

If you want to run one portion of script, you can go to script pane and select a particular portion of script. On the file menu, you can hit "Run selection" on your tool bar and hit run.

On the tool bar, you will get an option to stop the operation or you can also hit CTRL+BREAK or hit stop operation on the file menu. You can press CTRL+C and it works well on an already selected text. You can copy function of your selected text easily.

Enter Script in the Pane

If you want to enter your script in the Pane, you have to move your cursor to the pane by hitting anywhere in the pane or go to your script pane to check menu.

It is easy to create one script and syntax coloring along with the tab completion. It will be a great experience because you can easily manage this text. If you want to find something in your text, you can write CTRL+F on Edit Menu and hit "find this in script.

You can press F3 as well on the edit menu to find subsequent in the script. If you want to find any text before your cursor, you can hit SHIFT+F3 on your Edit menu and hit search previous in your script.

Search and Replace Text in Your Script Pane

If you want to search and replace any text, you can hit CTRL+H on your Edit menu and hit replace in the script. You have to enter both of your text that you want to find and with which you are interested to replace it. You can press Enter.

If you want to move on a specific line in the text of Script Pane, you can press CTRL+G on your edit menu and hit "Go-to-line" and enter one line number.

It is easy to copy text in your script pane because in the script pane, you can select text and hit CTRL+C on your toolbar. You have to hit the icon available for copy or directly hit copy in the edit menu.

If you are interested to cut a particular part of script in the pane, you can hit CTRL+X on your toolbar or hit the icon available to cut or you can directly select cut on your Edit menu.

You can paste this text in your script Pane by pressing CTRL+V or hit your paste icon located on your toolbar. On your edit menu, you can hit paste as well.

To undo any kind of action in your script Pane, you can simply hit CTRL+Z or press undo icon or word undo on your edit menu.

To redo any kind of action in your script Pane, you can simply hit CTRL+Y or press redo icon or word redo on your edit menu.

Tips to Save one Script

If you want to save any script, you can simply hit CTRL+S on your toolbar or press the icon available to save or hit the word "Save" in the menu. The commands of PowerShell scripts are almost similar to Windows.

Save Script in Particular ASCII Encoding

The PowerShell can save new files of script by default as .ps1, .psd1 and .psm1 as BigEndianUnicode. If you want to save your script in a separate encoding like ANSI (ASCII), you can use Save As or Save method. There are a few commands that will help you to save your .ps1 script along with ASCII encoding.

```
$psise.CurrentFile.SaveAs("MyScript.ps1", [System.Text.Encoding]::ASCII)
```

If you want to replace the current file of script with the similar name and ASCII encoding, you can use the given command:

```
$psise.CurrentFile.Save([System.Text.Encoding]::ASCII)
```

This command will help you to encode your
current file.

```
$psise.CurrentFile.encoding
```

The PowerShell supports different encoding
options, such as BigEndianUnicode, ASCII,
UTF32, Unicode, UTF7, Default and UTF8.

Procedure and Commands of Scripts

Commands and Procedures of Script

The commands and procedures of script is the
base of PowerShell. You can get the advantage of
framework to create your scripts and add some
conditionals and loops to make it logical. Scripts
of PowerShell are text files with special
extensions of ps1. If you want to create one script,
you have to enter one bunch of commands in one
particular sequence in the notepad file. You can
save this file as .ps1 and the name should be one

friendly description without any space. If you want run the PowerShell script, you can enter the window of PowerShell.

You have to write the complete path including name of folder and file of the particular script, such as: **c:\powershell\myscripthere.ps1** .

If the script is located in the present directory and the console may use one period and backslash, such as: **\myscripthere.ps1** .

There is no special thing to create one script in the PowerShell. You can add commands as per your preferences. One script needs more than a single thing or you should write a script for it. The scripts are common in the information technology. The administrators often use login scripts for many years to get environments and desktops configured as per users with every log in. With the advancement in technology, it is possible to script anything, from metal installation of your operating system on the server to workloads on servers. It also includes server roles of file or installing exchange.

In order to write a script, it is essential to cover a few elements and there are a few phases for your assistance:

Phase 01: Variables

This phase is important to make scripts in a consistent way. This scripting will make your work easy to do things repeatedly. You can do similar action with the same command. Variables are known as holders and you can use them to put words, numbers, values and anything with them. These will always have one dollar sign in front of them. There are some variables for your assistance:

```
$name = 'Jon'

$number = 12345

$location = 'Charlotte'

$listofnumbers = 6,7,8,9

$my_last_math_grade = 'D+'
```

You should declare all variables with dollar sign and use any name for variable without any space in the name. You have to give space followed by equal sign and then given another space.

If you want to have text in the value of a variable, you should add one single quote on both sides of your text. You have to declare one variable without writing value and reserve the particular name. It proves helpful in the center of the developing than at other time.

You can add output of cmdlet and t is one cute moniker to refer the simple bit of your .net-based code and it is easy to execute it to return the result. If you want to list all procedures, you can use Get-Process command and the Get-PSSnapin cmdlet display current PowerShell snap-in to activate new functionality. If you want to calculate the actual number of cmdlets on your system, youc an use:

```
(get-command).count
```

You can declare one variable to store and it is known as:

```
$numberofcmdlets
```

You have to store the output in the variable of .count entry:

```
$numberofcmdlets = (get-command).count
```

PowerShell helps you to find out the present value of a particular variable and write its name in the prompt:

```
PS C:\Users\Jonathan> $numberofcmdlets
1141
PS C:\Users\Jonathan>
```

This variable can be used as a part of anything else. For instance, look at the cmdlet write-host to simply script the text to particular screen of hosting machine in the PowerShell session. The Write-Host may have one bunch of proficiencies, but in simple manner, such as:

```
Write-Host "Whatever text I want, as long as it is inside double quotes."
```

You can copy this line in the window of PowerShell and you will see the actual results.

If you want the integration of variables with the Write-Host, you can write a dollar sign, such as:

```
Write-Host "There are $numberofcmdlets commands available for use on this
system."
```

You will get this from the PowerShell:

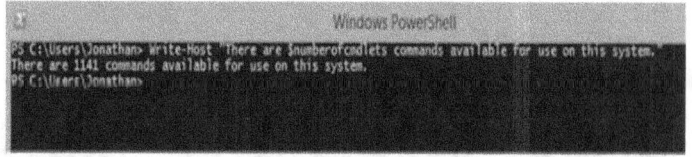

Phase 02: Do-White, If/Then and forEach

In the next phase, you will do some amazing magic, such as you have to store the value of variables.

If/Then

The simple form to make a decision in the PowerShell is the special if/then mechanism. It is called construct in the PowerShell lingo. It works in the particular way, such as:

If you want to do the comparison of something with something else, you can use this command.

You can format it with the help of parenthesis and put one curly brace alone on one new line. It is easy to add cmdlets or perform actions and if this action is the true beginning, you can write one curly brace on the new line. You have to cover the following points, such as:

There should be a logical retort of False or True. It is important to think about yes without any question. If you have to do something without yes or no, you should make a new loop and cover it in one bit.

If you have a yes/no statement, the code should run in the curly braces. It will be good to practice these braces on the line. You can match them on the place where you want to write complicated scripts. If you are interested to compare 2 numbers, 5 & 10, the PowerShell should display

that the 10 is greater than 5 and you can write
this script in the following way:

```
If (10 -gt 5)

{

Write-Host "Yes"

}
```

If you want to run the prompt of PowerShell, you
will get:

If you want to make one functional construct
with more nests, you can try this one:

```
If (10 -gt 11)

{

Write-Host "Yes"

} elseif (11 -gt 10)

{

Write-Host "This time, yes"

}
```

It will be easy to follow for everyone and see the given results:

```
PS C:\Users\Jonathan> If (10 -gt  11)
>> {
>> Write-Host "Yes"
>> } elseif (11 -gt 10)
>> {
>> Write-Host "This time, yes"
>> }
>>
This time, yes
PS C:\Users\Jonathan>
```

You can get different output with different values and names. It will be an easy way to manage functional scripts.

If you want bunch of blocks in your script, you can establish different conditions. You can select different blocks, but there is an example to make your work easy:

```
If (10 -gt 11)

{

Write-Host "Yes"

} elseif (11 -lt 10)

{

Write-Host "This time, yes"

} elseif (20 -gt 40)

{

Write-Host "Third time was a charm"

} else {

Write-Host "You're really terrible at math, aren't you?"

}
```

You can run this construct and get this result:

```
PS C:\Users\Jonathan> If (10 -gt  11)
>> {
>> Write-Host "Yes"
>> } elseif (11 -lt 10)
>> {
>> Write-Host "This time, yes"
>> } elseif (20 -gt 40)
>> {
>> Write-Host "Third time was a charm"
>> } else {
>> Write-Host "You're really terrible at math, aren't you?"
>> }
>>
You're really terrible at math, aren't you?
PS C:\Users\Jonathan>
```

Do While Examples

```
$numbers = 1
```

Then, let's set up a simple Do While construct that adds 1 to whatever number is already in that variable, until the variable has the number 10 in it.

```
Do {

$numbers = $numbers + 1

Write-Host "The current value of the variable is $numbers"

} While ($numbers -lt 10)
```

Run this script and your resultant command will be this:

You can set up one do while easy construct to set your commands for execution:

```
While ($numbers -lt 10) {

$numbers = $numbers + 1

Write-Host "The current value of the variable is $numbers"

}
```

You can notice different among image management in afore and after versions. All Windows PowerShell's version enables images to carefully share the layers. For instance, you can grab one image to share some similar layers of image as one image and it may be already pulled. The daemon Windows PowerShell can recognize this and pulls the required layers out of their stored location. The second pull proves helpful to pull images with common features and layers.

This illustration can help you, just start with 15.04 Ubuntu image that you have recently pulled and make some changes into it to build a new image. You can use Windows PowerShell build or Windows PowerShellfile command to make your work easy.

You can optimize resources by sharing them and people often do this impulsively in their life. For instance, Joseph and Jane are twins taking calculus classes at separate times from separate teachers. They can share their exercise book by passing it to each other. Jane has to complete the homework on the 11th page his book. Now, the original exercise book can't be changed and only Jane can copy this page.

Copy-on-write strategy is simple for copying and sharing. This strategy enables system (that requires similar data) processes the data instead of getting their own copy. At a particular point, if one procedure requires some modification to write data, only the procedure that should be written will copy the data. All other procedures will be continuing to the use of actual data.

Windows PowerShell requires one copy-on-write technology with containers and image. This strategy can optimize the performance of your container and disk space. In the next section, the system will work to leverage the copy with containers and images via copying and sharing.

Conclusion

Ethereum proves good to source funding and offers a legislative structure to get an exceptional idea. You can get proposals from other people who supported your project and hold votes on the possible procedures. It allows you to skip the expenditure of a conventional structure, such as completing paperwork and hiring managers. Ethereum protects a project from external influences, while it's decentralized network make sure to avoid any downtime.

There are numerous small aspects that make both blockchain-based projects different. Average block time of bitcoin is almost 10 minutes, but the Ethereum aims for 12 seconds. This instant time is enabled by the GHOST protocol of Ethereum. A quick block time indicates that confirmations are quick. There can be more orphaned blocks. Another difference is the monetary supply of both cryptocurrencies. More than 2/3rd of bitcoins are already mined with the majority going to initial miners.